Questions and Answers About RTI

A Guide to Success

Heather Moran
Anthony Petruzzelli

Eye On Education
6 Depot Way West, Suite 106
Larchmont, NY 10538
(914) 833-0551
(914) 833-0761 fax
www.eyeoneducation.com

Library of Congress Cataloging-in-Publication Data

Moran, Heather.
Questions and answers about RTI : a guide to success /
by Heather Moran and Anthony Petruzzelli.
     p.   cm.
ISBN 978-1-59667-183-6
1. Response to intervention (Learning disabled children)
2. Slow learning children—Education—United States.
3. Learning disabled children—Education—United States.
I. Petruzzelli, Anthony.
II. Title.
LC4705.M67 2011
371.90973—dc22   2011006169

10 9 8 7 6 5 4 3 2 1

Acknowledgments

No educational endeavor of the magnitude of a Response to Intervention model could ever succeed simply with the vision of a small group of people. The current RTI model in place at Gloucester Township Public Schools has been an effort of many people. Some members of the administrative team that were important to its initial inception have moved onto other districts, and some current critical members have joined in the effort in progress. We wish to acknowledge the support of the GTPS Board of Education and central administration and applaud the efforts of the "front line troops" that administer the screenings, provide the interventions, manage the progress monitoring, and keep the belief in the system alive. We especially would like to acknowledge the building administration who have helped shape and sell "the message", provide the leadership at the building level , and always do what is best for the children in their charge.

We also wish to acknowledge the support and encouragement of our families and friends. This was an undertaking that started out unassumingly as an idea in a department meeting and grew to a level where we believe we have good information to share to help students across the country. This cannot happen without people believing in you and pushing you forward. Thank you, everyone . . .

Meet the Authors

Heather Moran earned a B.A. degree in elementary education from Rutgers University. She holds an M.A. in educational leadership from Wilmington University and completed an M.S. in mathematics education at Rowan University. Heather has taught 5th and 6th grades in elementary school, middle school mathematics, and has been an elementary school assistant principal. She is currently an instructional supervisor in Gloucester Township Public Schools in Camden County, New Jersey.

Anthony Petruzzelli has B.A. degrees in systems analysis and elementary education from Rutgers University. He holds an M.A. in educational leadership from Rowan University and completed his Ed.D. at Seton Hall University. Anthony has taught at the middle school level, been an elementary school assistant principal and principal, and is currently the assistant superintendent for curriculum and instruction in Gloucester Township Public Schools in Camden County, New Jersey.

Table of Contents

Preface vii

1   **What is RTI, Anyway?** 1
    Individuals with Disabilities Education Act (2004)
       and Response to Intervention 2
    This Acronym Makes Sense! 4
    RTI and the Discrepancy Model 4

2   **Why Try Something Different?** 7

3   **How Did Our District Make the Change to an RTI Model?** 13

4   **What Are the Core Beliefs of Response to Intervention?** 21
    The 7 Core Beliefs 21
    Selling the Message 25

5   **What is the Three-Tier Model?** 27
    Our Model vs. the "Classic" Model of RTI 30

6   **What is Universal Screening?** 35
    Universal Screening Tool Selection 35
    Universal Screening Tools 37
    Oral Reading Fluency and Reading Comprehension 38
    Using the Universal Screening Data 39
    Identifying Students Who Are "Potentially At-Risk" 40
    Ensuring Enough Service for Identified Students 41
    Universal Screening—Not the Only Way In 42

7   **What is Progress Monitoring?** 45
    Tools 46
    Frequency 46
    Data Collection 47
    Target Line Identified 47
    Growth Line Plotted 48
    Response to Intervention Trend Determined 48
    The Power of the Visual 50
    More on Middle School and Progress Monitoring 51

8 Who is the RTI Team and What Do They Do? .53
RTI Team Members 53
Data Collected for Meetings 56
The RTI Meeting 56
    RTI Team Decisions. 60
Fidelity of the RTI Team 62
RTI Team vs. Other Student Improvement Teams 62

9 What Happens in Tier 1? 65
What Happens in Tier 1 66
Tier 1 Doesn't Come in a Kit 66
Creating Your Own Tier 1 "Kit" 69
Ensuring Intervention Fidelity 70

10 What Happens If In-Class Interventions Aren't Enough? 73
How Does a Student Get Into Tier 2? 73
What are Tier 2 Interventions? 74
What Tier 2 Interventions Should Be 77
A Story of Struggling Kindergarteners. 80
System Responsibilities of the Interventionist 81
Can In-class Support be a Tier 2 Intervention? 82

11 What Happens if Tier 2 Doesn't Work? 85
How Does a Student Get Into Tier 3? 85
What are Tier 3 Interventions? 87
What Tier 3 Interventions Should Be 87
Multi-Disciplinary Team Involvement. 89
What Happens if a Child in Tier 3 Shows
    an Inadequate Response to Intervention? 90
A Word on Retention. 91
What if They Don't Qualify for Special Education Services? 92

12 How Do I Get Started in My District? 93
Decisions Specific to Middle School Implementation 99

13 How Can I Apply RTI in Other Areas? 105
Behavior Modification and RTI. 106
Other Academic Areas and RTI. 107
Upper-Elementary Grades and Beyond. 109

Preface

This is a book about a journey—a journey to recognizing that we can do better for our struggling students by creating a structure that maximizes our resources and ensures that every student gets the help they need as early as possible. Response to Intervention may just be the structure that maximizes the efforts of many dedicated educators who desperately wish to ensure the success of every child. Have you had students "fall through the cracks" and who have been moved through school without the critical skills they need to succeed? We believe that RTI holds the answer to that. Have you had students that you feel become intervention "gold-card holders," that is, students who see a basic skills teacher or Reading Specialist in first grade and are still seeing them in eighth? We believe that RTI eliminates this. Have you had students who had to "wait to fail" before they could receive necessary help? We believe that RTI prevents this from happening. It may sound too good to be true, but it is not "too good to be true" for several reasons. RTI is a great deal of hard work. It may solve the aforementioned problems, but it certainly is not easy. The school must undergo cultural shifts for it to succeed. It will challenge long-held beliefs, and the district must provide a significant amount of professional development. Teachers, principals, and central administrators must weather the tough times to reap the benefits. Further, RTI is not a program, but a structure. In many ways it is a belief system. It does not prescribe specific interventions or methodologies. Instead it creates the structure (with a strong foundation of data) to ensure that students receive the level of attention they need as quickly as possible. You cannot "do" RTI as if it were a packaged program. However, as districts "fill in the blanks" with their instructional materials, trainings, methodologies, and personnel, the overall scope takes the shape of a program. We occasionally use the term "program" in this book. At times, we use it to describe a scope that is more than just a structure, but the heart of this book is about creating that structure so that you can "fill in the blanks" with your own resources. Finally, RTI relies on the best tool available in schools: the expertise of teachers. The RTI structure will ensure that every child gets the attention he or she needs without supplanting the teachers' expertise; the better the teacher, the better the RTI efforts will be.

This book is intended to provide a "road map" for a successful RTI implementation. It is light on numbers and heavy on practical examples and straight talk. It is designed to guide a school or district through the implementation of a new RTI program. It is also meant to provide an easily understandable "manual" for teachers who are being asked to provide service in an RTI structure. If you are an elementary educator, much of what we have written will speak directly to you. The examples and tools are mostly from elementary school experiences. If you are a middle school administrator, please do not close the book just yet. There is much to digest here for any educator. Even though most of our examples are based in elementary school settings, the core beliefs and the essential understandings we discuss and describe in these pages translate to any grade level and to almost any student concern. What is important is the belief that early identification, aggressive intervention, consistent progress-monitoring, and a willingness to alter interventions can address a variety of concerns. We believe that reflection on these concepts will help bring RTI philosophy to elementary, middle, and even high school levels.

We started an RTI initiative in our school district before we knew that this acronym existed. As the RTI program in our district grew, we began to discuss our efforts with neighboring districts and soon began to present our practices to other school administrators and teachers. The book is based on those presentations. For this reason, we write as we would present: with true stories of what we have seen. We tell you what we did, what worked, and what didn't. We tell you about the obstacles we faced and how we addressed them. We share our successes and our failures. By doing this, we hope that you will benefit from our experiences and gain a deeper understanding of what you face. It has been well worth the journey. RTI was a "rocky road" for us, and still has its critics, so we keep trying to improve on it. But it has been very beneficial for our students, and that truly is the bottom line. If you are reading this, we assume that you are about to embark on this journey yourself—either as a central administrator, a principal, or a teacher. We hope to help you along the road.

Note

We use the term "Child Study Team" often in this book. This term can have different meanings depending on the state in which you work. In New Jersey, the Child Study Team consists of a school psychologist, a learning disability teacher consultant (LDTC), and a social worker. The Individuals with Disabilities Education Act (IDEA) defines the team of people that determines if a child has a specific learning disability as "a team of qualified professionals including at least one person qualified to conduct individual diagnostic examinations of children, such as a school psychologist, speech-language pathologist, or remedial reading teacher." Such a team may have a different name in your district such as Individualized Education Program (IEP) Team, Student Intervention Team, etc. The group that we are referring to when we say "Child Study Team" is the group or individual responsible in your district for processing a referral for special education testing and carrying out that testing procedure. Please keep this in mind as you read, and translate "Child Study Team" into the term that you are familiar with in your district.

1

What is RTI, Anyway?

Every profession has its own language—words and phrases that set it apart from all others. Education is certainly no exception. In addition to numerous words and phrases, the educational world seems to have a unique affinity for acronyms. It can border on humorous to sit in a meeting with educators and count how many different acronyms can be used to identify one issue or problem. But as frustrating as these acronyms can be to outsiders, they often refer to important ideas and issues. A popular one in our circles right now is RTI, and it absolutely fits the criteria of an important idea with the potential for amazing results with our country's struggling students.

RTI stands for Response to Intervention. It is an intervention model in which a teacher identifies potential challenges for students as early as possible, intervenes immediately, and adjusts the intervention as needed until the student progresses at a rate that will close any identified gaps. While the model is most often applied to academic struggles, particularly those in the area of language-arts literacy, the model has a far-reaching scope and can be applied to almost any problem at any level.

RTI relies on data-driven decision making. While teachers certainly know their students strengths and weaknesses and should always listen to what their "gut" says, it is vital that our profession bases important decisions like intervention on data that can be supported by research. The identification step is accomplished by a Universal Screening mechanism that provides such data quickly and accurately. The interventions are adjusted based on accumulated data that is gathered to monitor the student's progress towards the goals. This data guides all future decisions ensuring that all students are treated equally and have access to the same quality interventions.

RTI also relies on research-based practices. The interventions chosen should have proven, research-based track records. These interventions are to be delivered by well-trained instructors, both classroom teachers and specialists.

Many times, the educational world is at fault for simply purchasing materials for teachers, often ones that are showy and attractive, and not following it up with sustained, job-embedded professional development. Teaching is a difficult job, especially when it comes to assisting those students who are struggling and need more assistance than the materials being used for the masses can provide. Interventionists need materials with a proven track record, and then must be taught how to use them most effectively. This training needs to be supported over time and done with constant consideration of the specific attributes of the person's job. It is not an easy task, but the payoff is worth it.

Again, it is easiest to see RTI as an intervention model for academic concerns in young children. However, the concept of identify early, intervene aggressively, monitor effectiveness, and alter intervention as necessary, can be applied to any concern—academic or behavioral. Educators can change the way they approach issues in their schools and be much more successful overall.

Individuals with Disabilities Education Act (2004) and Response to Intervention

The popularity of the term "Response to Intervention" exploded when it received great attention in the 2004 reauthorization of the Individuals with Disabilities Education Act (IDEA). With increasing dissatisfaction in the discrepancy formula approach to identifying students with learning disabilities, the prominent mention of an alternative approach in this important legislation caught the attention of many. The 2004 reauthorization of IDEA provides an alternative approach to special education classification when it states, " . . . When determining whether a child has a specific learning disability as defined in § 602 (29), a local educational agency *shall not be required* [emphasis added] to take into consideration whether a child has a severe discrepancy between achievement and intellectual ability . . . In determining whether a child has a specific learning disability, a local educational agency may use a process that determines if the child *responds to scientific, research-based intervention* [emphasis added] as part of the evaluation procedures . . . " The 2004 legislation also allows local educational agencies (LEAs) to designate up to 15% of their IDEA allocation for pre-referral programs to intervene for students and prevent classification. This does not mention RTI specifically, but a Response to Intervention model is just that—a model to intervene and prevent classification by providing intensive services prior to the referral process. The use of RTI as a classification process also makes perfect sense. You know that you have a struggling student so you do everything you can to help. At some point, the classroom teacher's resources and all of the school's resources have been used up. You have tried everything. Assuming that you've tried it all with the highest degree of integrity, what is left to do if the child is still struggling? Doesn't it make sense to say, "We have done everything we can pre-referral, now we need special education"? This explains some of the dissatisfaction with the discrepancy model, which is often called a "wait to fail" model, because schools and teachers feel that they must wait for a child to do poorly over a period of time before they can "get help". The IDEA reauthorization allows LEAs to use an RTI model as a classification process and also provides funding to programs for struggling, yet unclassified, students. Consider the following example, which is representative of hundreds of kindergarten classrooms across the country.

> Erin is a five–year-old girl who has arrived in kindergarten at her neighborhood school for her first academic experience. Erin's young parents did not have the means to send her to preschool and while she sings the alphabet song and can recognize some letters, she is not sure of many letter sounds and she has trouble writing her name. She is an eager student who wishes to please the teacher, and her parents are willing to put in extra efforts at home if the teacher shows them how.

Erin is obviously behind her peers in the classroom. Many students arrive in kindergarten knowing all of the letters and the accompanying sounds, the basic color words, and some sight words. The key question in this example is: What is the best course of action for Erin? Is it best if the teacher simply treats Erin as she does everyone else and only seeks out special education services if Erin falls far enough behind? Or, is it better to begin to intervene often with research-based materials and give Erin the best possible chance to catch up to her peers academically? Obviously this example is extremely simplified, but the key features happen over and over again across the country. Erin, and all the students like her, deserve the opportunity to be as successful as they can be *prior* to a special education classification becoming a necessity.

Before this becomes a discussion of special education classification, we must emphasize that, while it was IDEA that put Response to Intervention "on the map," RTI should not be seen as a special education initiative. The entire RTI process happens pre-referral and outside of any special education classrooms and programs. Identification in an RTI structure is meant to allow for immediate intervention. Testing, in the form of progress monitoring, is meant to assess the effectiveness of the intervention and guide decisions in altering intervention programming and intensity. RTI is designed to ensure that every possible option has been aggressively explored *prior* to a special education process referral.

This Acronym Makes Sense!

RTI: It will roll off the tongue very easily after you say it several thousand times. But this acronym really has something of value to say. RTI stands for Response to Intervention. As you read this book, you will see that those three words are the key to the entire program. Every student that needs additional help, all of the time that teachers spend with struggling students, the interventionist staff that is hired specifically to help with struggling students, the meetings, the forms, the computer programs . . . it is all about the Response to the Intervention. Once a student is identified as potentially at-risk, the RTI process begins. The teacher makes deliberate efforts to address the student's struggle. In other words, the teacher *intervenes*. They intervene with specialized centers, specific group work, individualized homework, and other tactics. Then, the student's *response to the intervention* is measured. Are the interventions working? Should we change them? Should we intensify them? If the student does not show adequate response to the intervention, they may move on in the process. A specialist begins to see the student and supplements the classroom teacher's efforts. The specialist uses research-based programs to help the student. Again, they *intervene*. Again, we measure the student's response to the intervention over time. We ask the same questions to determine how to best help the student. What is the Response to the Intervention? By constantly measuring the student's response to the intervention, we ensure that we have the opportunity to constantly adjust our efforts until we know we are seeing the progress that we want.

RTI and the Discrepancy Model

While it certainly seems that the process of exhausting all general education resources prior to classification makes RTI a logical alternative to the Discrepancy Model of classification, a strong word of warning must be made. The discrepancy model relies on sophisticated testing, administered by experts in learning disabilities, to determine if a child qualifies for special education services. These tests have a long and solid history of research and practice behind them. We have all been frustrated by the "wait to fail" aspects of the discrepancy model. However, an established RTI program that has testing validity, intervention integrity, and sufficient resources at its disposal to supplant the discrepancy model, will be years away from an RTI program that is just starting. Great care must be taken to establish valid testing protocols with research-based testing materials, to provide strong professional development in the diagnosis of and intervention in students' academic challenges, and to develop a secure system of procedures to ensure program integrity and fidelity. It is our very strong recommendation that a Response to Intervention model be implemented with a special education *referral* as the last resort, not a special education *classification*.

Response to Intervention is, at its heart, not about special education classification at all. It is a general education initiative designed to identify potential issues early, and to intervene aggressively on behalf of those students so that they may enjoy learning in the least restrictive environment and also meet their greatest potential.

2

Why Try Something Different?

Change is never easy. Sustaining the status quo is comforting. The known, even if it has inadequacies, is easier to deal with than the unknown. All of these statements describe why it is often difficult to look for something different when faced with a structure that is not working. In many school districts across the country, the structure for assisting struggling students is a perfect example of this. To begin the difficult process of change, the primary stakeholders in the school need to identify concrete reasons why a new perspective on the issue could benefit everyone involved.

For many school districts, a good starting place is to investigate how struggling students are identified, and how this identification leads to the assistance that they require. Districts commonly find that teachers recommend struggling students for intervention simply because the students' grades are not up to par. While teacher input is certainly an important component for identification, simply relying on grades to determine who needs additional support can lead to an inequitable system of access to remedial assistance. The inequity comes from an absence of data-driven decision making. Classroom grades are not a uniform measure of achievement no matter how closely teachers work together because personal preferences and biases impact how assignments are graded. Also, some teachers are more willing to seek outside assistance for their struggling students, while others prefer to handle it themselves. Using standardized data to decide who gets access to intervention services levels the playing field by ensuring that every student is judged by the same criteria. When a school bases decisions on data, such as in a Response to Intervention model, all students and teachers are treated equally. It is less about being a right or wrong issue and more about equitable access. Response to Intervention models are therefore a great alternative to systems of intervention based on less regimented information. If a school is not using data to determine who receives intervention services, it is imperative to look for something different.

While this reliance on data to make decisions seems as if it should be intuitive to educators, it is often very far from the status quo in public schools. Before the advent of easy-to-use technology, gathering and manipulating data was time consuming and difficult. Classroom teachers did not have routine access to computers, and any data that was finally available generally arrived long after instructional decisions had been made and carried out. Today, teachers have more access to computers and there are a plethora of options available to assess students. Schools looking to change the way they identify struggling students need to make sure that their instructional leaders are making these options available and accessible to classroom teachers. These leaders also need to be able to articulate the advantages of using such a system as opposed to simply relying on the classroom observations of teachers. It is so important to remember how difficult change is for professionals who already have challenging jobs to perform. Building-level leaders must show the relative advantage of changing the way struggling students are identified if they expect teachers to alter their behavior.

Progress monitoring is another aspect of a Response to Intervention model that encourages educators to search for something different. Once students have been identified as needing remedial assistance, another challenge begins. How does one know if the remediation is actually working? In many intervention situations, classroom grades are the only yardstick used to measure the progress of the child. If the classroom grades are improving, the belief is that the intervention is working. While this may be the case, we know that grades are not always a clear measure of academic ability. Grades tend to take into account a multitude of factors, not just the skills that need remediation. It is easy to understand how teachers want to reward an increase in hard work and dedication a student may be making. This change should absolutely be rewarded, but it doesn't necessarily translate into improved skill. A Response to Intervention model selects a research-based progress monitoring tool to chart the growth a child is showing in particular areas directly related to the academic deficiency being addressed. The results of this progress monitoring allow educators to make clear decisions about the effectiveness of the remediation and make changes as necessary. Again, the playing field is leveled for all teachers and students, and judgments about progress are made by looking at consistent information. Schools that are not currently using a research-based progress monitoring tool may want to consider looking to redesign their approach to accessing their intervention services.

A classic example illustrating the need for a regimented progress monitoring system is the student who struggles with comprehension. Imagine a typical elementary school that is using an anthology based reading program in the upper elementary grades. A teacher may identify a student as needing assistance because the student is not producing high grades on the end-of-selection test for the week's anthology story. The identified student typically sees a Reading Specialist or other interventionist a few times a week for half-hour sessions. It is very common for these sessions to revolve around reading and re-reading the anthology story in a variety of settings. Perhaps the adult reads the story aloud to the student, or the student partner reads with another classmate, or the student listens to the story on tape. All of these interventions will most likely lead to higher scores on the end-of-selection test, and therefore to better grades in the classroom. However, the question that needs to be asked is whether or not the student's comprehension is improving. If the remediation is deemed necessary to improve comprehension, then the student should undergo a comprehension assessment to see if the remediation is indeed improving the child's ability. Progress monitoring allows educators to detach their assessments from classroom grades and objectively look at the skill in question. Keep in mind that if the intervention is working and the student is progressing, classroom grades will ultimately improve. It isn't that RTI discourages concern for the child's grades. The difference is that the improved grades are the result of improved skill, not just a result of increased attention to the particular story. The ultimate goal of an RTI model is to improve the areas in which the student is lacking, thereby making the child a stronger student overall. If the model is successful, classroom grades will improve, as will standardized test scores and other assessment measures.

Imagine a typical middle school classroom. The opportunities for supplemental instruction decrease as schedules get more regimented. The elementary school classroom offers some opportunities for supplemental instruction, but the middle school schedule makes it so much harder. Consequently, middle schools often resort to supplanting instead of supplementing. Educators end up grouping students with different challenges together and try to meet all of their needs. We know from extensive research that this is counter-productive. "Extra help" in the form of after-school tutoring and other efforts often help a student pass a test, improve a grade, or pass a course, but has genuine remediation occurred? Will the student be more successful on his or her own on the next test or the next course? Imagine a structure that encourages and supports supplemental assistance so that a student can remain in a regular classroom setting. Further imagine that that assistance is designed to genuinely close skill gaps and ensure that the student will be better able to succeed independently. Progress monitoring at the middle school level helps ensure that precious supplemental time is used effectively and helps target interventions to specific concerns. As in the elementary school example, targeted interventions monitored for their effectiveness will improve skills and abilities that will have positive impacts far beyond the current assignment or class.

Progress monitoring reflects a second important reason to consider looking for an alternative method of making intervention services available to students. Many times, either the student or the teacher is blamed when intervention services do not result in observed improvement. Some educators may say that the student is simply not working hard enough, and others may say that the teacher is not providing the intervention services with enough fidelity. Either of these scenarios may be true, but educators often overlook the idea that *the intervention itself* may not be suitable for the student's issue. Monitoring the child's progress as remediation occurs allows the intervention to be changed as soon as inadequate progress is shown. Changing the intervention and continuing to monitor progress allows educators to look at the intervention itself as the reason that progress was not demonstrated. This eliminates the need to blame the child or the teacher, and places the emphasis on looking for a different method or tool that can enable the child to succeed. The ultimate goal of remediation is to find the best match between the intervention being delivered and the student being serviced. Progress monitoring allows this relationship to take center stage. Consider this real life example that is similar to the theoretical situation discussed before:

> Janet entered one of our elementary schools in first grade. She had gone to a private kindergarten the year before, which was her first school experience. While Janet was able to name all her letters and identify the majority of their sounds, she entered first grade as a true non-reader. Her classroom teacher worked with her and her parents throughout the first part of the year, but by the winter break, Janet had been referred to the school's Reading Specialist. Since this was pre-RTI in the school, the Reading Specialist accepted Janet into the intervention program based on the teacher's request and started seeing Janet three times a week. The Reading Specialist focused on helping Janet prepare for the end of selection tests and Janet's classroom grades improved dramatically. The classroom teacher and Janet's parents were very pleased with her progress. The intervention continued throughout the year, and at year's end Janet's grades were good enough to dismiss her from the intervention program. This scenario was repeated again in second and third grade, each year seeing Janet's grades plummeting early and requiring the services of the Reading Specialist. Now Janet is in fourth grade and the same chain of events has unfolded. Janet has become an intervention "gold-card holder"—she is never ready to be permanently dismissed from the program.

The key element to take away from this example is that Janet's comprehension problem was never adequately addressed. The Reading Specialist helped her improve her classroom grades and perform better on the end-of-selection tests, but her comprehension never improved. If Janet were in first grade now, the work she would do with the Reading Specialist would be progress-monitored, and if she did not show acceptable improvement, the tactics used would be altered. This process would continue until the comprehension issue was solved, or until it was deemed that she required services outside the general education realm.

The reason to adopt a different means for identifying struggling students centers around the students themselves. The goal of a Response to Intervention structure is to improve student achievement and to make the students more successful academically. The structure also strives to make sure the students are actually getting the intervention they need to remediate their academic deficiencies, as opposed to simply getting more instruction that does not impact their success. A true Response to Intervention program does not allow students to continue to receive assistance that is not productive. Therefore a student who enters a basic skills program in the first grade will not receive comparable services in the fifth grade without changes occurring in the meantime. These basic skills program "gold-card holders" no longer exist because changes are continually occurring in the prescribed program if the struggling student does not exhibit adequate progress. Students either make progress or the plan of attack is altered.

This same idea of monitoring progress is expressed by the 2001 legislation *No Child Left Behind*. One of the four main principles of this legislation is accountability for results. It is no longer acceptable to judge a student's progress on classroom grades alone. A teacher needs to be able to unequivocally show that what he or she is doing in the classroom is working. A Response to Intervention model supports this goal of accountability by looking at objective data to make decisions. The data can be compared within a particular grade level and across schools to make decisions such as whether or not a specific intervention is working for a particular student or if a school- or district-wide program is achieving the desired results. Teachers are able to make informed decisions that impact instruction in a positive manner.

While *No Child Left Behind* legislation requires schools to compare student achievement to a grade level benchmark, it is equally important to monitor students' personal growth. Many times, a student is unable to demonstrate adequate progress when compared with peers in the same grade level. While achieving at this level should remain the goal, it is important to document and celebrate the individual progress a student makes against him or herself. This is another definitive reason to include progress monitoring as part of a solid intervention structure for struggling students. Parents, teachers, and students need to have access to a consistent means of documenting personal growth. It is important for the self-esteem of the child, and it is equally important to gauge how well a specific intervention program is actually working.

Change is never easy. It is difficult to try something new especially when you are dealing with an institution as complex as a school. Response to Intervention is worth the time and the effort because the rewards are immeasurable. Student progress is placed at the forefront and is monitored closely so success is inevitable. The growing pains required to make the change occur are well worth the effort.

3

How Did Our District Make the Change to an RTI Model?

To have a true understanding of the change process associated with adopting an RTI model, it is helpful to understand what our district has encountered on our journey thus far. Our suburban district is located in southern New Jersey, and services approximately 7,700 pre-kindergarten through eighth grade students. The district is comprised of eight elementary schools, whose grades levels range from pre-kindergarten through fifth grade, and three middle schools with grades six through eight. While the percentage of students living in poverty varies from school to school, the district average is about 30%. The eleven schools also vary in racial and ethnic make-up with each school embodying its own unique personality. These factors, combined with the schools' wide size variation, created distinctive challenges as a new RTI philosophy was introduced and ultimately adopted.

As with many new ventures in the twenty-first century, our journey began with a Google search. Terms like "Response to Intervention," "progress monitoring," "pyramid of intervention," and "curriculum based measurement" were appearing all over educational literature. The common links connecting these terms seemed to mirror the underlying intervention philosophy that the district aspired to have regarding intervention services for struggling students. The information gathered led to the creation of a district-wide committee convened to guide the district as it moved forward. This committee was comprised of central office administrators, building-level administrators, Child Study Team members, and classroom teachers. The goals for this committee were not large in number, but their scope was expansive. The team of educators was asked to:

- ◆ Define the district RTI philosophy
- ◆ Create the district RTI model that would guide decision making
- ◆ Select the Universal Screening and progress monitoring tools
- ◆ Define Tier 1, Tier 2, and Tier 3 interventions
- ◆ Create an implementation timeline

The decisions made to satisfy each of the categories above would significantly change the way struggling students received services in our district, so the task was not to be taken lightly. Although significant change is difficult, it is often necessary. The committee understood this fact and began the journey by identifying the key points of our RTI philosophy.

Outlining a philosophical statement for a district is similar to creating a mission statement for a school. Most of the time the majority of the organization's members implicitly understand the beliefs and guiding principles of the group, but when it comes to articulating them on paper, the waters tend to get a bit murky. This was certainly the experience of the committee presented with the task of defining the key ideals of a new RTI protocol.

The first necessary statement in the philosophy seemed apparent to all the members of the committee. For years, teachers and parents in the district had expressed concern over the length of time that had to pass prior to a student receiving supplemental services for academic difficulties. It was commonplace for students to have to "wait to fail" before action could be taken. RTI provided an alternative structure that identified potential academic concerns as early as possible. The benefits of this decision had far-reaching impact. The committee was especially pleased with the word "potential" when used to refer to academic concerns. Too often educators place an inappropriate label on a student and make it extremely difficult for him or her to change it. An RTI model proposes that the foundation of any successful intervention program should allow for the earliest possible identification of an issue and the ability to remove that identification if deemed appropriate. This idea of early identification became the first tenet of our new intervention model, and truly became the cornerstone around which every other decision was based.

The next attribute of the philosophy did not come to fruition as easily. The educators working on the project became bogged down easily when deciding which materials or strategies to use for an RTI program rather than focusing on ideals to frame a philosophy. Our profession often looks for the next "quick-fix" for a problem and assumes that it will come prepackaged. Although this was a difficult hurdle to overcome, it became a strong foundation of the new RTI structure. Once they identified a potential academic concern, teachers would intervene immediately with research-based best practices. This meant that struggling readers did not follow one prescribed set of steps. Student A might have been placed in Tier 1 because she struggled with the initial sounds of words presented to her. Student B might have been placed in the same tier because he struggled with phoneme segmentation. While both of these students exhibited reading difficulties, the materials that will help them the most are not identical. Each of these students needs an individual program tailored to his or her particular issues. Prescribing one intervention (or even one set of interventions) to suit all Tier 1 students was just not practical. While many teachers debated this tenet when the RTI structure was unveiled, it has proved to be a very important decision that has supported many other core beliefs.

The committee continued to debate issues surrounding the development of an RTI structure and developed three more core beliefs (for a total of five). While it might appear that these ideals are relatively simplistic and easy to agree with, the process to develop them into concepts that would guide a district's access to intervention services was not at all easy. The committee met several times over the course of four to six months to settle on the philosophical foundations that would guide the RTI model. The tenets that guided all future decision making were as follows:

- ♦ Identify potential concerns as early as possible
- ♦ Intervene immediately with research-based best practices
- ♦ Monitor student progress often
- ♦ Determine student response to the intervention being provided and intensify as needed
- ♦ Seamlessly integrate Special Education services and General Education interventions as classification simply becomes the "next tier" of intervention after all pre-referral efforts have been exhausted

It was time to take the foundational principles and develop a functional model that would allow the ideas of RTI to play out with actual struggling students in the district. Philosophical guidelines are important and useful, but the day-to-day implementation has to be well thought out so that educators can carry out the process with integrity and fidelity. The structure developed had to support the carefully conceived ideals while also allowing multiple school buildings to execute it easily.

The committee again turned to outside research to guide discussions about creating a workable structure for implementing the RTI principles they developed. The model in its entirety is discussed in much greater depth in Chapter 5, but it is important to demonstrate the integral role the philosophical statements played in the creation of actionable events. First, the committee decided that the district would benefit from having three levels (or tiers) of pre–special-education referral interventions. This let educators address potential concerns as quickly as possible while emphasizing that remediation could potentially correct the deficiency and that a special education referral might not be necessary. The committee felt very strongly that this belief take prominence in both philosophy and practice. In this district, it was uncommon to believe that pre-referral interventions could work and ultimately allow a struggling student to close their academic gap. Interventions were seen as a means to improving classroom performance. While that is certainly a worthy goal, it does not always match the ultimate measure of success, which is improving a child's ability in the area of the deficiency.

Another key component of the model was that a student's success in any tier would be examined through Progress-Monitoring tests given over an eight-week period, and the unique trends found in the data collected would be the basis for subsequent decisions. Regularly tracking students' progress outside of traditional classroom assessments was a foreign concept to the great majority of personnel who would be implementing RTI. The reliance on data to drive decision-making became a crucial component of the model. This complete process was illustrated in an easy-to-follow flowchart so that all district employees could obtain assistance for struggling students following the same parameters.

The journey toward a complete and cohesive RTI model continued with the decision to adopt DIBELS as a Universal Screening and progress monitoring tool. DIBELS stands for Dynamic Indicators of Basic Early Literacy Skills, and it was developed at the University of Oregon during the 1970s and 1980s. These tests look at a series of foundation skills that can predict a child's future reading success. Each test or probe is one minute in length and is administered individually to students by a trained professional. The scores on these probes are entered into a database that tracks progress and makes recommendations regarding the need for intervention services for students.

Many decisions should impact the selection of a Universal Screening and progress monitoring tool. Our decision-making process was based on three key areas: time, ease of use, and cost. The committee insisted that the product selected must be one that took relatively little time away from instruction, that the staff could easily manage, and that was cost effective, as it would be an investment that would continue for an indefinite amount of time. Many programs claimed to meet the group's three most important criteria, but none seemed to meet them as well, or have as much research to support them, as University of Oregon's DIBELS project. As mentioned before, the probes are one minute in length each, and the only cost is one dollar per student that the University of Oregon charges for managing the data that teachers input. Teacher training seemed to be an obstacle that could be overcome as well, so the tool selection was complete.

Once the governing committee finalized these major decisions, other administrators and teachers were brought up to speed with the progress made toward a comprehensive RTI system. These administrators and teachers spread the information to all teachers who would be impacted, and an entire school year was spent practicing the components of the newly drafted RTI structure. Teachers universally screened students and selected some of the students who were identified as struggling for Tier 1 placement and progress monitoring. The data collected throughout this first year was analyzed to make decisions about the model's effectiveness, but it was not used to impact decisions made about any individual students. The eventual success of our RTI program was greatly affected by this decision to simply practice for an entire year prior to actual implementation. Too often, educators expect immediate results from a newly purchased or executed program without providing staff members with adequate training and transition time. The time spent "practicing" with the RTI components allowed all the decisions to solidify into a cohesive model that would serve our students well.

A crucial aspect of the model that was mentioned previously addressed the specific interventions that would be used at each tier of the RTI model. Many staff members—both teachers and administrators—wanted a step-by-step approach to the use of interventions. The feeling was that Tier 1 should have a list of interventions that was different than those listed for Tier 2 and so forth. The "practice" time helped the committee determine that the teachers who were providing the intervention had to have a great deal of autonomy when it came to selecting the intervention to be used in a given situation. It became apparent that well-trained interventionists (in our case, Reading Specialists and basic skills instructors) and classroom teachers were the ones who should be determining which materials to use for which students. Certainly the frequency and intensity of the interventions had to be uniform across schools, but the actual intervention used had to be dictated by the type of difficulty the child was having, not necessarily by the tier he or she was in. While this seems like a very common sense approach, it really is different from the way many educators approach problems. Since a school is an institution, those that govern the institution find it necessary to prescribe particular responses to specific problems. This cannot always be the case when working with children, especially those that are facing academic struggles.

A final issue that has plagued us from the very beginning of our journey is comprehension. A direct link exists between a child's ability to read fluently and his or her ability to comprehend what he or she is reading. That said, there are certainly students out there who are fluent word callers and have no idea what the words that they decode mean. While DIBELS does have a reading comprehension component with its screening materials, the committee decided that our staff could not become comfortable enough with it to depend on it for decision-making. After the RTI model had been in operation for some time, a second means of entering the intervention structure emerged.

In the beginning, the committee saw the DIBELS screening as the only means of access to Tier 1 and, therefore, to intervention services. The issue of comprehension led to the creation of the Request for Review of Records form. This form lists all the data that had been collected on a student, from DIBELS scores and guided reading level, to standardized test scores and classroom grades. This form, completed by the classroom teacher, could be submitted to the RTI team who could in turn recommend that the student enter the RTI system as a Tier 1 student. More specifics regarding this procedure will follow in later chapters, but it is important to note that the district continues to make improvements to the RTI structure as more and more students pass through the system. It truly is an ever-evolving journey.

Perhaps the most telling aspect of our journey is the story that has become something of an RTI mantra for us. The young boy at the center of this vignette truly became the face of RTI for all involved and reminded everyone of why the journey was so vital.

Shawn arrived at a district elementary school and enrolled in second grade at the start of the school year. After a few days had passed, his teacher came to the assistant principal of the school with genuine concerns. Shawn was a nonreader. Even more alarming was the fact that he did not seem to have the same concepts of print as his peers. His interest level was much lower than his classmates' and his behavior was becoming a consistent problem. The guidance counselor at the school became involved, quickly suggesting that the teacher bring the student to the Intervention and Referral Services (I&RS) team so that interventions could be administered to help Shawn.

As the teacher and the guidance counselor gathered the data required for the I&RS meeting, it became evident that Shawn's problems extended far beyond his reading difficulties. Shawn had been in five schools prior to starting second grade in our district. Shawn was living in a single-parent household with his father and often had to go to his father's place of employment after school. His attendance was a concern at each of his previous schools, and his grades and report card comments drew a bleak picture. It was obvious that as a toddler or primary grade student, Shawn had not had the necessary exposure to the basic elements of reading. The question became what to do about all of that now that he was a second grader.

The I&RS meeting brought together the school administrators, the guidance counselor, the Reading Specialist, the nurse, the speech teacher, a building special education teacher, and Shawn's classroom teacher. His parent had been invited to attend, but was unable to come. The meeting began with Shawn's teacher explaining what was happening in the classroom and how difficult it was for her to provide the services that Shawn seemed to need. After reading through his records and listening to the observations of the teacher, it became increasingly evident that Shawn was a student who suffered from some environmental disadvantages. He had not had the same exposure to basic early literacy that many of his peers had, and this problem was compounded when combined with his poor schooling experience.

At the same time this I&RS meeting was occurring, the district was in the "practice" year of RTI. The Reading Specialist and the building administrators at Shawn's school were very involved in the district RTI plans, and they believed that Shawn was the perfect candidate for intensive intervention with consistent progress monitoring. Shawn was placed in Tier 3 and immediately began seeing the Reading Specialist individually for one hour every day of the week. At first, some people thought that this was an excessive use of the interventionist's time. But over the course of the next few months, Shawn began to show significant progress in his reading ability. In fact, by the end of the year, Shawn was reading at grade level and was performing well at classroom activities with very little modification.

The moral of this story is very clear. Shawn did not have a true learning disability and did not need the benefits of a traditional special education classification or program. It is important to remember that he probably would have been deemed eligible for services under the discrepancy model for classification. Child Study Team members would have found a discrepancy between his ability level and his performance in the classroom, and he would have found his way into a resource center setting. Shawn did not need all of these services. He simply needed targeted instruction in his areas of deficiency and his academic gaps would close.

Our RTI journey has always been about helping students like Shawn. The goal has been to make sure that the right students are classified and receive the appropriate special education services they require. Students without true learning disabilities certainly need interventions, but they are separate from those provided by our special education peers. The core beliefs of RTI make sure this occurs.

4

What Are the Core Beliefs of Response to Intervention?

With any new program in any industry, it is essential that those delivering the new procedure believe in its potential to be better than current practice. The structure of a strong Response to Intervention model keeps the parts moving, provides rules to administrate, and has guidelines to follow. However, the underlying engine that makes an RTI model grow more effective each year comes from the core beliefs that district staff members have rallied around. The ultimate goal is to have these core beliefs become part of the school culture. The degree to which any school has already embedded such beliefs in their culture will change from district to district and building to building. However, it is crucial for any administration attempting to create an effective RTI model to realize the critical nature of having a common set of core beliefs take hold within the staff. This is something that has to be deliberately planned and executed; such beliefs have to be internalized, not legislated.

From the standpoint of a district administrator, building administration and teaching staff must internalize these core beliefs. The person or people bringing a Response to Intervention model to a district or building must constantly guard against the RTI model simply becoming a process to follow, forms to fill out, and a series of "hoops to jump through" to get to a Child Study Team evaluation. Response to Intervention is far more than a structure or procedure. It is a core set of beliefs about how struggling students can be remediated.

The 7 Core Beliefs

Educators must understand that struggling students can be helped without special education services. RTI interventions are all pre-referral attempts to remediate problems while keeping a child in the general education classroom and exposing him or her to the core curriculum. In order for any pre-referral services to be most effective, it is critical to find the children who need help as early as possible. Therefore, the first core belief of Response to Intervention is to *identify struggling students early.*

One of the greatest criticisms of the discrepancy model for specific learning disability (SLD) determination is that it is a "wait to fail" model. Students have to demonstrate that their struggles are having an educational impact (i.e. they have to be failing before intervention is warranted). Response to Intervention requires that educators seek out students with challenges that will *potentially* result in academic struggles. This does not ask teachers to be able to identify learning disabilities or to be able to distinguish them from developmental delays. It is also not asking for a system in which the "gut feeling" of an educator is the gatekeeper to interventions. Rather, it requires a research-based, data-driven approach of screening every child early and often to predict future learning challenges.

By identifying students who have the potential for future academic difficulties early, there is no reason to wait for frustration or failure to begin intervening. The second core belief of Response to Intervention is to *intervene immediately with research-based programs* in order to address identified difficulties.

Once students have been identified as potentially at-risk for future academic struggles, intervention should begin immediately. Current procedures in most classrooms have this step regardless of the existence of a Response to Intervention structure in their school. Every teacher, from the first day of school, is on alert for the student who may be struggling. Once identified, the teacher usually intervenes immediately. Classic interventions would include working with the student one-on-one during some classroom down time or during independent work time. Teachers will provide additional assistance in the form of varied activities during the school day, the placement into a group to work on a specific skill, or the creation of special centers for the student. Differentiated instruction is, by its very nature, intervention for identified students. A strong Response to Intervention belief structure couples the idea of early intervention with the practice of early identification.

In addition to believing that early intervention is essential, RTI supports the belief that such intervention should always occur in the least restrictive environment. The goal of RTI is to remediate deficiencies before they have significant educational impact. A least restrictive environment is not only better for the emotional well being of the child, but it ensures that the student continues to work "on grade level" with full exposure to grade level materials, content, and expectations while remediation is occurring. Another essential component of the early intervention belief is that such interventions should be research-based and that the teacher should be adequately trained to deliver them effectively. RTI is a data-driven intervention model and the integrity of the intervention delivery is critical to the success of the program.

While the first two beliefs probably exist in most classrooms across the country, the third begins to separate the RTI model from the norm. With screening tools or simple observation, teachers identify the students in their classes that may need "extra help," and they begin to give that help. However, there is rarely any method of determining if the intervention is successful in remediation of the problem. There must be a procedure for determining if the efforts made, the materials used, the intensity shown, and the interventions chosen are effective. The third core belief of Response to Intervention is to *monitor progress regularly* to gather necessary data. Teachers need immediate and regular feedback to determine if the intervention being used is successful. This must be accomplished by the use of a valid measure, regularly taken over time. A great criticism of "high stakes" testing is that it is an entirely summative, single "snapshot" of performance. It provides no information to act on immediately and cannot report growth because tests are usually given near the end of the school year, with results arriving after the students have left for the summer. Monitoring student progress each week with a standardized, valid tool gives a teacher valuable information while the intervention is in process. With weekly data gathering, teachers and schools will see trends, and will be able to react accordingly.

The progress-monitoring data, gathered over time, will give a strong indication of the intervention's effectiveness. The fourth core belief of Response to Intervention is to *determine the response to intervention* to make decisions about the next steps. With weeks' worth of data from a valid measuring assessment (administered by a trained teacher) reflecting an intervention being made with integrity, a school-based team can make an informed determination regarding the student's response to the intervention. The only question that really needs to be answered is: Is it working? Often, interventions are given in the form of "extra help." Sometimes they are programs in the classroom, sometimes they represent additional help outside of the classroom, and sometimes they are in the form of after-school clubs or tutoring. Maybe an upper grade "buddy" has been assigned to drill flash cards. Perhaps a student sees another staff member in a small setting during the school day. Maybe the student comes to the teacher to review homework before the school day begins, or the student could work with the classroom teacher right after lunch each day during silent reading time for the class. All of these may be good ideas. All of these scenarios certainly happen in schools across the country. But how do we know if what we are doing is working? How do we decide if we should continue with these methods? How do we know that this is a good investment of resources? With progress monitoring data in hand, school-based teams can answer the question: Is it working?

When the answer is "Yes," the next steps are easy. Keep doing it, it's working! But when the answer is "no," action must be taken. The fifth core belief of Response to Intervention is to *change or intensify the intervention as needed*. When the answer to "Is it working?" is "No," there must be an acknowledgement that the intervention (not the child, not the teacher) has failed and needs to change. Perhaps the intervention itself needs alteration, or perhaps it needs to be implemented more often or for longer periods of time. It would be similar to your doctor prescribing medicine to you. If you take the medication over time and your symptoms do not improve, your doctor did not fail you. Instead, there is an acknowledgement that the intervention (the medicine) has failed in its task, and something must change either in practice (new medicine) or in intensity (higher dosage). In the same way, addressing failed interventions prohibits us from allowing too much time to pass without the student making genuine progress.

Many traditional intervention models involve only the classroom teacher and special education. Often the only option in between is "extra help," which can simply become tutoring sessions to prepare for tests instead of genuine attempts to remediate. If this has been the culture of the school, then not only do the teachers believe that this is the sole approach, but also the parents do as well. During the first years of a new RTI structure, it will be a common perception that it simply delays an inevitable special education referral. That is why the process must be discussed with all of the stakeholders. The sixth core belief of Response to Intervention is *open, transparent communication among all stakeholders*. Teachers need to know that their students have the necessary interventions available to them, and parents must know that RTI provides more intervention, and does so earlier, than the current practice.

The seventh and last core belief is a culmination of the first six: *Special education and general education are seamlessly integrated*. Think about the process of special education in your school or district. There are levels of intervention ranging from minimally intensive and least restrictive to greatly intensive and very restrictive. You have students in your classrooms that have Individualized Education Programs (IEPs) for in-class support, in which the students remain in a regular classroom with minimal accommodations. They use the general education materials, and they are responsible for the general education work. Students needing more intensive intervention could be placed in a resource center environment where their program has been modified to use different materials from the general education materials, and in which the students have different goals than their peers. Students who may need more intensive intervention than this could be placed in self-contained programs that are more restrictive and have greater accommodations. Some students cannot be accommodated for within the walls of your school, and they may be placed in another school outside of the district. This is the most restrictive and most intensive of interventions. Special education is ruled by assessments to determine placement, to set and adjust goals, to review progress, and to alter program. All such program decisions are done with the full knowledge and consent of the parent. Response to Intervention is not new, philosophically, to special education staff. By extending this educational philosophy to the general education population, we can take the best of the two education models and seamlessly integrate them. Consider the special education interventions as simply the "next steps" when other interventions fail. You can see the seamless integration of general education and special education where simple classroom interventions are on one end of the intervention scale and self-contained special education programs are on the other with everything in between available for every child. This creates one united staff, not a general education staff and a separate special education staff, that works together to ensure the best program for every child.

To review, the core beliefs of Response to Intervention are:

1) Identify early
2) Intervene immediately in the least restrictive environment with best practices
3) Monitor progress regularly
4) Determine response to interventions
5) Change/Intensify intervention as needed
6) Have open communication with teachers and parents
7) Create a seamlessly integrated system of interventions

Selling the Message

Some, if not most, of the described "beliefs" seem so obvious that it is hard to imagine that they need to be emphasized so much. But, despite their logic, they are often very far from regular practice in most schools. In our experience, we have run into many schools (including our own district, years ago) that would not classify a kindergarten student. Some won't even bring them to a student intervention team. Some schools do screenings, but often only for placement purposes, not early identification. Yet progress monitoring, the determination of RTI, and the changing of interventions cause the real divergence. So often, as we noted in Chapter 3, students become intervention "gold-card holders." Dependent on the extra help that they receive from interventions, these students are never truly remediated and must continue in a more restrictive environment indefinitely just to survive academically. To formally place a student in something called "Tier One" immediately changes the approach to that student. With progress monitoring, there is an accountability piece that didn't exist before. The idea of determining "intervention failure" is also foreign. The best thing an RTI proponent in a school has is the logic of the core beliefs. Yes, they run contrary to current practice in many ways, but they are difficult to argue against when taken piece by piece. The RTI proponent has to recognize this strength and sell the message. In our district, we call it "preaching." Some perceive that word negatively, so you may not want to use it. But we took every opportunity to stress the core beliefs—in administrator meetings, in teacher meetings, in Child Study Team meetings, during chance meetings in hallways—we took every opportunity to sell the message. "If this child is going to struggle, let's find out now!" "How do we know that what we are doing is working?" "If it isn't working, let's not wait—let's do something different!" These messages connect strongly to the Response to Intervention model and are so difficult to argue against. A good RTI proponent will use them to their full effect.

Having staff members who believe that the aforementioned steps are the best way to identify and assist every student in need of help is only half of the Response to Intervention equation. The other half, the RTI structure, provides the guidelines and administrative rules that support the RTI core beliefs and allows them to flourish. The next chapter provides a brief overview of the structure, which will be studied in detail in the following chapters.

5

What is the Three-Tier Model?

Response to Intervention is based on the core beliefs of identifying problems early, intervening immediately, monitoring progress often, and making the necessary changes to the interventions being provided. All of these steps are designed to help the struggling student achieve more success in the least restrictive environment possible. In theory, these are all traits that educators can rally around. Intellectually supporting these beliefs is not difficult, but putting them into practice requires structure and protocol. A three-tier Response to Intervention model provides the organization necessary to move educators from a place of idealistic theory to one of concrete action.

Before you can look at each of the pieces of the Response to Intervention model in detail, you must have an understanding of the process as a whole. Figure 5.1 on page 28 outlines the model in its entirety, and describes how struggling students move within the system. Subsequent chapters will provide greater detail about each aspect.

A basic tenet of Response to Intervention is the belief that educators must identify struggling students early. The three-tier model begins with a Universal Screening of all students three times per year. While we will discuss the selection of a tool for Universal Screening at length in a future chapter, it is important to note that this diagnostic test is given to all students regardless of academic level. The goal of this assessment is to identify the students who are "potentially at risk" for developing academic difficulties. These children officially become Tier 1 students.

The classroom teacher provides in-class Tier 1 interventions to the newly identified students over an eight-week period. Tier 1 Interventions may include additional small group time, differentiated instruction, learning centers, extra home activities, and classroom modifications. In essence, Tier 1

FIGURE 5.1 Standard RTI Model

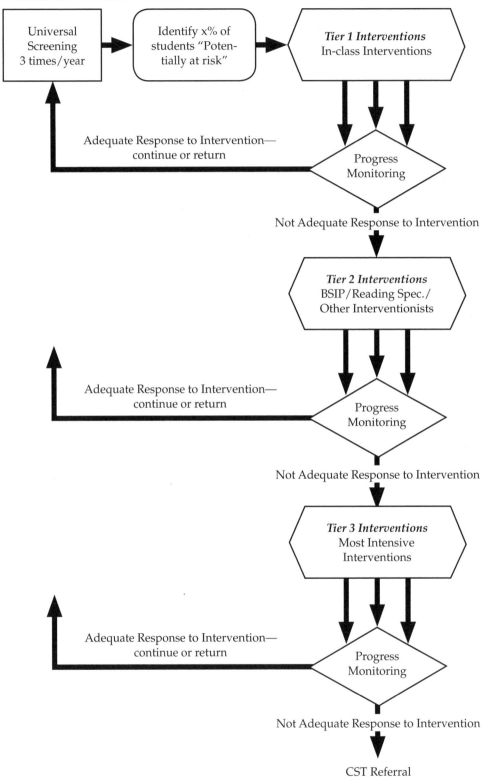

interventions are the cornerstones of good teaching that exist in classrooms all across the country every day. The structure supplementing this good teaching is twofold. First, the students receiving these interventions have been formally identified by the Universal Screening process. The mere act of tagging these students as Tier 1 makes the classroom teacher more aware of their needs. Heightened awareness leads to more attention, which in turn will benefit the student. Second, the classroom teacher is now responsible for progress monitoring the Tier 1 students to see if the classroom interventions have acceptable results.

Progress monitoring is done through the use of probes. Probes are short diagnostic assessments designed to track student growth during an intervention period. These probes should mirror the Universal Screening tool and should also be easy to administer. Classroom teachers give each Tier 1 student a set of probes once a week during the eight week intervention period. The teacher charts probe scores on a graph and eventually the scores begin to show a trend. Educators looking at the graph will decide if the student is, in fact,"responding to the intervention." If the student's scores show a positive trend, the educators may decide that the student can remain successful as a Tier 1 student. This would mean that the interventions would continue and the classroom teacher would continue to monitor progress. In other cases, the response to the intervention may be so great that the educators feel the student can leave Tier 1 altogether. In still other cases, the trend may not be positive at all and educators looking at the graph may feel that the student needs more intensive interventions in order to succeed. If this is the conclusion, the student moves to Tier 2.

Tier 2 students are tagged only after there has been a lack of adequate response to intervention in Tier 1. Tier 2 students are not identified as a result of doing exceptionally poorly on the Universal Screening. Tier 2 students are identified **only** after the interventions in the least restrictive Tier 1 have failed to produce adequate results.

Once a student enters Tier 2, they begin to receive interventions outside of the regular classroom. An interventionist will now provide services to supplement what is occurring in the regular classroom. An interventionist can be a basic skills instructor, a Reading Specialist, a corrective reading instructor, or any other certified staff member without primary classroom responsibilities. Ideally, interventionists are those with the most extensive training in the area that is to be remediated. In Tier 2, the interventions usually occur every other day in small group settings. For example, a typical Tier 2 model would have a child seen in a group of four to six students, 30 minutes at a time, two or three days a week. The interventions are in addition to what is already occurring in Tier 1 inside the classroom. These Tier 1 interventions do not stop simply because another professional is helping the child. The responsibility for the child's success is now simply shared with another teacher.

Tier 2 also lasts for an eight week period. During this time, the interventionist administers the progress monitoring probes since they now provide the primary source of intervention. The educator continues to administer the probes weekly and the results are added to the graph started in Tier 1. Again, the educator is seeking a response to intervention trend. If the trend is generally positive, the student may be kept in Tier 2 for an additional eight week session. If the trend is so positive that the student could sustain an intervention reduction, the student may be returned to Tier 1. If the trend does not illustrate enough response to intervention, the student may be moved to Tier 3.

Tier 3 interventions are the most intensive offered within the three-tier model. These interventions are again administered by an interventionist outside the regular classroom. A typical Tier 3 plan would have the student seen individually or with one other student, four to five times a week at 45–60 minute intervals. Reducing the group size, increasing the frequency of the intervention, and lengthening the intervention sessions greatly intensify the intervention. The interventionist still monitors progress, and the classroom teacher continues to provide Tier 1 modifications even though he or she is no longer responsible for progress monitoring. Tier 3 interventions continue for an eight week period with the progress monitoring probes recorded on the graph once a week. After the eight week session is complete, the educators look for trends on the graph. A student with a strong response to the intervention may either stay in Tier 3 or go back to Tier 2. If the student shows no response to intervention, then the child is referred to the Child Study Team for testing and a possible special education classification.

It is important to note that each tier is structurally similar to the rest. The differences exist in the type of intervention provided at each level. The intensity of the intervention changes quickly between tiers and the staff person responsible for the progress monitoring varies, but the organization of the tiers and the decisions made at each level are very similar. This creates a seamless transition for students and teachers as individual students move around in the model.

Our Model vs. the "Classic" Model of RTI

A three-tier model is not unique in Response to Intervention literature. Many authors, including Brown-Chidsey and Steege (2005), and Wright (2007) refer to three- part systems that increase a student's access to progressively

FIGURE 5.2 Common RTI Triangle

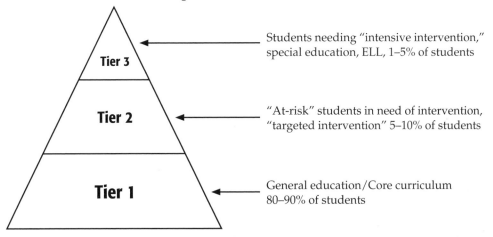

Tier 3 — Students needing "intensive intervention," special education, ELL, 1–5% of students

Tier 2 — "At-risk" students in need of intervention, "targeted intervention" 5–10% of students

Tier 1 — General education/Core curriculum 80–90% of students

more intense interventions after the student has been identified as need-ing assistance. While these models share many common characteristics, it is important to note significant differences. It is essential to look at these few vital aspects when deciding what type of model would most efficiently meet the needs of a particular school setting.

Buffum, Matos, and Weber (2009) and Burns and Gibbon's (2008) mod-els identify Tier 1 as the general education curriculum, therefore they place all students in Tier 1. This is a model that seems common within many RTI programs. You may have seen graphics that look like Figure 5.2 in published programs or other written works.

Perform an internet search for "RTI triangle" and you will quickly see many different versions of this, but most will have similar language, similar percentages, and similar definitions for each tier. We recognize that many experienced educators support the above structure, but we admit that we are puzzled by several implications of such a structure. First, identifying Tier 1 as the general (or core) curriculum establishes nothing new and certainly does not offer struggling students any advantages. We assume that every school has a core curriculum that they are either confident in or are working on that is designed to address local goals, as well as state and national standards. We assume that every school encourages differentiated instruction within their classrooms, and has trained teachers who work with individual students. If these systems are not in place or are not in the process of being established, they are additional issues that the school district needs to address. This book is about adding an effective and efficient structure to identify, address, and monitor the needs of struggling students. We further assume that every school already has a system for intervening with struggling students. We treat RTI as an intervention model that brings structure to current intervention processes.

We approach RTI as a model that supports data-driven decision making, efficient use of resources, and effective timelines. We also believe that a good RTI structure will minimize the need for special education services, thereby reserving them for the students who truly need them. The RTI triangle that we often observe, like the one above, restates the need for a strong core curriculum and differentiated instruction in the classroom. By defining Tier 1 this way, this "classic" model misses an opportunity to provide a greater level of intervention in the least restrictive environment. Further, by suggesting that Tier 3 includes special education, this model's three tiers become: 1) general education, 2) pre-referral intervention, and 3) special education classification. This is not revolutionary, and it does not provide the essence of an RTI model, which requires that interventions increase in intensity based on the student's response.

Our model, by contrast, assumes a strong core curriculum exists, and that teachers are trained in differentiated instruction techniques. If we were to translate our model into an RTI triangle graphic, it might look like Figure 5.3.

Our model, as described in this chapter, differs from the arrangement shown in Figure 5.2 because it identifies Tier 1 as *the first line of intervention*. Students need to be identified early through mechanisms like the Universal Screening process. If the screening identifies some students as "potentially at risk," those students begin to receive extra services from their regular classroom teachers. These services are in addition to those provided to the student population at-large, and are meant to supplement the general education curriculum. The decision to identify Tier 1 in this manner relates to our core beliefs about Response to Intervention. Students need to be identified early, as they are by the Universal Screening, and intervention must happen immediately in the least restrictive environment possible, as they are by receiving additional assistance from their primary teacher in the regular classroom. Interventions must happen immediately and in the least restrictive environment possible, which means students should remain in their regular classrooms and receive additional assistance from their primary teachers. Labeling Tier 1 the "regular education" curriculum means that a struggling student's first intervention above the core curriculum happens outside the primary classroom in a more restrictive Tier 2 environment. In our model, that same struggling student would receive his or her additional intervention within the classroom. The decision to provide instruction of any kind outside the regular classroom should never be taken lightly. Providing the first level of interventions within the primary classroom setting ensures that this will not happen.

A second vital aspect to consider is where Tiers 2 and 3 will fall in relation to special education and the referral process for such services. In the model

FIGURE 5.3 Our Model as an RTI Triangle

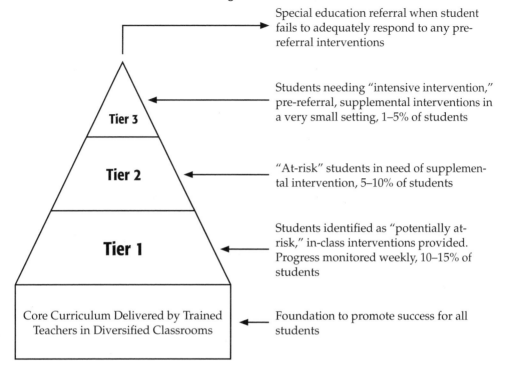

we illustrate in this chapter, all tiers are pre-referral and occur within the general education realm. Again, this relates to the core belief that interventions should occur in the least restrictive environment. Some models suggest that a lack of response to the interventions that the tier system provides should automatically lead to a special education classification. While this may be the eventual outcome for many students who fail to show adequate response to Tier 3 interventions, our model (outlined above) leads only to a Child Study Team referral. When this referral occurs, the Child Study Team begins the traditional battery of tests to determine special education classification. A lack of adequate response to intervention at Tier 3 does not automatically trigger a special education classification.

Our three-tier model provides structure and organization to the seven core beliefs of Response to Intervention. While the tiers share commonalities in construction, they vary greatly in the type and intensity of interventions offered. They are bound together by the belief that all struggling students deserve to receive interventions in the least restrictive environment possible, and that teams of educators should use data to determine the most appropriate interventions. The next chapter begins a discussion of each part of the model in greater detail beginning with Universal Screening.

6

What is Universal Screening?

The Universal Screening is a key component of an RTI model that is efficient, effective, gains the support of the school staff, and earns the confidence of the school community. The screening is the gateway to the entire RTI process and is a key to quickly helping students who need it while utilizing staff efficiently. Despite the critical nature of the data collected via the Universal Screening, the tool selection process needs to focus on more than just a reliable outcome.

Universal Screening Tool Selection

There are a plethora of options available to a school district that is selecting an assessment tool to be used as a universal screen for their RTI system. There are existing assessments in textbook series, commercial products made specifically for Universal Screening, and programs with built-in assessment systems, such as Fountas and Pinnell's *Guided Reading* programs. In selecting your tool, you should focus on these five characteristics: amount of supportive research, ease of use, assessment time required, cost, and clarity of outcome definition.

Amount of Supportive Research Universal Screening will require a great time investment. Certified staff who would otherwise be teaching will have to take time to assess hundreds of students multiple times during the year. This is a huge price to pay, so the data had better be worth the time spent. The screening's results will indicate which students should be selected for intervention, and that will take even more of the professionals' time. The time allotted to provide these interventions should be scheduled based on accurate information. Therefore, take deliberate steps to ensure that the screening tool that you select has a strong research base. Was it designed to do what you want it to do? Have the results been validated in research studies? Upon what research foundations does the program rest? These are critical questions to answer to ensure that the time invested produces reliable data.

Ease of Use Any certified staff member should be able to administer the tool easily. In our model, any teacher who does not have primary classroom responsibilities—meaning anyone who is not a classroom teacher—can perform the Universal Screening. Reading Specialists, basic skills instructors, speech teachers, resource center teachers, and others will all assist in the Universal Screening process. If the tool is easy to use, training the staff will be simpler and the tool's delivery will be more consistent. This will enhance the validity of the data. An easy-to-use tool will also promote greater staff acceptance.

Assessment Time Required An elementary school of 600 students cannot have a Universal Screening tool that takes each student 15 minutes to complete. It is simply not practical. More time will usually mean more detailed and more reliable data, however the purpose of the screening is to find out as much as possible, as quickly as possible. When selecting a tool, the time required to assess each student is a critical component. You want it to be fast and accurate. When the population that you are testing becomes more targeted, your diagnostic testing can be more detailed. Upper-elementary and middle school students may be able to undergo computerized screenings. This may speed up the process and make the collection of data easy, but it also may be unnecessary. By the time a student reaches the upper-elementary or middle school grades, you will have a wealth of information available to you. Grades, standardized test scores, previous RTI data, anecdotal data, and other data will have accumulated. At this stage, a universal "paper" screening of existing data may be just as effective in identifying students in need of assistance as another test, but without the added time investment.

Cost In public schools, there will always be a cost concern. Commercial products with extensive materials and online tools (such as color graphs and fancy reports) can become very, very expensive. It is also been our experience that many of these, particularly those with computerized data tools, are subscription-based products. This means that you will be incurring costs every year for your RTI data warehousing. We have seen subscription-based products that are as low as $1 per student per year, and as high as over $20 per student per year. There are additional costs if you are buying materials.

Outcomes Clearly Defined Once the product has been purchased, the training concluded, and the staffing investment has been made, you want to have clear direction regarding the students who you have screened. Again, teachers and Reading Specialists will always do more detailed diagnostic testing to direct the tools and tactics that will be used to help a child, but the Universal Screening is meant to be easy, quick, and clear. The tool should provide definitive direction for students and make a clear distinction between students who are "at-risk" and students who are not.

In short, the Universal Screening tool should be valid, easy, and inexpensive; should take little time to administer; and should provide clear results. We liken it to casting a wide net. The idea is to catch as many students as you can while investing as little time and money as possible. The goal is to be as accurate as possible while being very aware of the classroom instruction time that teachers lose when they are conducting assessments.

It is important to note that the purpose of Universal Screening is to identify students who are *potentially* at-risk. This is different from an aptitude test, a summative test, or an end-of-course selection. Typical testing in class occurs after instruction has taken place, and it assesses students' ability to demonstrate mastery of taught skills or content. This will highlight concerns for students who have not learned the material presented. The Universal Screening is meant to highlight *future* concerns, so that instruction may be targeted and intensified as needed before a student fails a course, performs poorly on a summative test, is retained, or is classified as needing special education services. In order to do this successfully, Universal Screening tools assess foundation skills, as opposed to complex skills built on foundation skills. Thus, the screening is designed to predict future concerns instead of identifying existing concerns.

Universal Screening Tools

There are numerous forms of Universal Screening tools available for purchase. The National Center on Response to Intervention has a summary of many of the available tools on their website at www.rti4success.org. There you will find a "Screening Tools Chart" that gives the Center's review of several popular tools, including DIBELS and AIMSweb. This chart provides an excellent overview of the varied programs available, but you will need to do additional research as you investigate individual programs more extensively.

When evaluating a tool, you need to consider another critical question: Which grade levels will be universally screened using this tool? There is a logical progression that leads to this question. If the purpose of the entire RTI system is to catch potentially at-risk students as early as possible, then the earlier we can screen, the better. Why, then, isn't Universal Screening in kindergarten sufficient? The answer to that is in the developmental nature of children. Kindergarteners will show up in September of their first schooling experience and have a very wide range of abilities, confidence, talents, and social skills. Over the course of their first few years of school, many of these developmental differences disappear or become much less pronounced. By only screening students in kindergarten, you run a great risk of missing those who have difficulty "keeping up" as the challenges of first and second grade approach. But, in recognizing the instructional time cost of Universal Screening, isn't there a time when the low number of new students identified through such screening fails to make the investment worthwhile? We believe there is such a time, and we further believe that time is at the end of third grade. Most Universal Screening tools would have you continue past third grade with their products. However, we feel that the enormous expense of instructional time lost to administer a Universal Screening outweighs the benefits starting in fourth grade. Universal Screening is inherently about information gathering. By fourth grade, a school has accumulated an enormous amount of information regarding a student, including four years of Universal Screening data, classroom assessments, grades, and standardized test scores. The school has also accumulated four years' worth of observation and evaluation by professional staff. There is no simple screening tool on the market that will provide more valid information than all of that combined. Therefore, after third grade, the Universal Screening can stop and other means of identification can replace it, provided that the school or district creates alternate ways for move-in students and students who develop difficulties after third grade to enter the RTI system.

Oral Reading Fluency and Reading Comprehension

There are many scholarly works that strongly support the case for using a measure of oral reading fluency to gauge a student's reading comprehension. In an article entitled "Oral Reading Fluency as an Indicator of Reading Competence: A Theoretical, Empirical, and Historical Analysis," Lynn Fuchs, Douglas Fuchs, Michelle Hosp, and Joseph Jenkins (2000) examine studies and other works regarding the connection between oral reading fluency and reading comprehension. Their article proposes:

... that oral reading fluency represents a complicated, multifaceted performance that entails, for example, a reader's perceptual skill at automatically translating letters into coherent sound representations, unitizing those sound components into recognizable wholes and automatically accessing lexical representations, processing meaningful connections within and between sentences, relating text meaning to prior information, and making inferences to supply missing information. That is, as an individual translates text into spoken language, he or she quickly coordinates these skills in an obligatory and seemingly effortless manner, and because oral reading fluency reflects this complex orchestration, it can be used in an elegant and reliable way to characterize reading expertise.

This is a complicated proposition that they discuss in detail in their article, and it is a proposition on which most Universal Screening and progress monitoring tools "hang their hats." As detailed in the article, there is a strong and lengthy history of research to support the contention that oral reading fluency is a confident predictor of reading comprehension ability. We are confident in the work of those researchers who have come to this conclusion, and we direct you to their works should you need more convincing.

Using the Universal Screening Data

The key to Universal Screening is *universal.* That means *every* student in the grades identified is screened using the tool three times a year. This is a great investment of time and there is the temptation to omit future screening for students who perform well on the first screening. There are several reasons for continuing to screen everyone throughout the school year.

First, as mentioned before, just as a child's academic development cannot be broken down into years, so it cannot be broken down into Universal Screening blocks that happen multiple times during a year. A student who scores well on an initial screening is not forever immune to academic difficulties, just as a student who performs poorly is not condemned to eternal challenge. Continuing to gather standardized information at regular intervals over a long period of time will help minimize any "falling through the cracks" potential.

Second, gathering thousands of data points over time provides a wealth of reliable information to a school and a district. If you have 100 students at a grade level, and you screen three times a year from kindergarten through third grade, you gather 1,200 data points in a single year. Over a short time, you will have thousands of data points, which makes the information more and more reliable. You can use this body of data to assess program decisions on varying scales. On a small scale, teachers can assess the effectiveness of individual centers as they see data trends for students of varying abilities over long periods of time. On a larger scale, schools can assess the effectiveness of programs that use significant resources. How much more prepared are Transitional First students for first grade than their kindergarten counterparts? Do those gains continue through second grade? Such data could help answer those questions. Perhaps the principal institutes a reading club during recess for students who want to stay inside. The screening data could help assess if such self-selected, volunteer reading time positively impacts fluency and comprehension.

Third, Universal Screening provides growth data for students who are not placed in a tier. This will account for over 80% of the students in most classrooms. Schools and districts are investing a great deal of professional time, instructional time, and money to create "benchmark" assessments to provide such growth data. The Universal Screening tool is already a research-based tool that is being faithfully implemented in the school. The data gathered can certainly supplement, or even replace, some benchmark assessing.

Fourth, the Universal Screening data will provide comparative data between classes and across schools. Anytime you use a standardized data-gathering tool across classes and schools with the same material support, you will be able to use that data to assist in diagnosing classroom or school specific concerns.

Identifying Students Who Are "Potentially At-Risk"

The main reason for the Universal Screening is, of course, to identify students who will be placed into Tier 1 interventions. As mentioned at the beginning of this chapter, the goal of the screening is not to determine students' aptitude for previously taught material. The goal is to identify students whose foundation skills leave them vulnerable to current and future challenges.

After the administration of the Universal Screening, the scores are reviewed, either through a computer program or by hand, to determine which students failed to reach a set benchmark. Those who reach or surpass the set benchmark are not identified. Those who do not reach the benchmark are identified as students potentially at-risk, and they are formally placed in Tier 1. The Universal Screening tool that you select will undoubtedly have pre-determined benchmarks for your use. For example, one popular Universal Screening tool uses the term "Benchmark" to describe a student who is comfortably over the required score; "Strategic" to describe a student who meets the benchmark, but could have some difficulties; and "Intensive" to describe a student who needs immediate intervention. This third category, "Intensive," would be the students identified as Tier 1 students. The information gathered on other students is still valid and can assist a teacher in making grouping decisions, center-assignment decisions, and other decisions about their academic interactions with students. Once these "Intensive" students are officially "Tier 1" students, the procedures for intervening, progress monitoring, and reporting will be followed by the classroom teacher, which ensures that the RTI structure remains intact.

Ensuring Enough Service for Identified Students

Any school or district has limited resources. There is certainly research that spells out which students are at-risk, and which students need additional intervention outside of the general curriculum. However, the number of students who can receive additional services (particularly in Tiers 2 and 3 which require additional staff) will be a function of the human resources available at any given school. Because of this, there is no magic formula that we suggest using to determine how many students will qualify as Tier 1. The number of students identified as Tier 1 will certainly impact the number of students moved to Tiers 2 and 3, which will, in turn, put pressure on staffing and schedules. To address this and ensure that a) you do not identify more students than you can serve, and b) that you do not *under*-utilize your intervention staff, we recommend the following procedure:

1. First, use the benchmarks set by the creator of the Universal Screening Tool. If you have selected your tool well, it is research-based and has a proven track record. The benchmarks they set will be valid.

2. Recognize that about half of the students identified as Tier 1 may move to Tier 2 and that a fraction of them may move to Tier 3. Note that Tier 2 students can meet in groups of four to six students for 30 minutes every other day. Tier 3 students meet in groups of one to three students and meet for 45 to 60 minutes every day.

3. Proceed through the first year of RTI being as faithful as possible to the screening benchmarks and the tier movement decisions.

4. As the year progresses, you will begin to get a sense of the resources required to provide Tier 2 and 3 interventions, and whether or not you have those resources available. If the answer is, "Yes, we have enough resources," then continue with the benchmarks. If the

answer is "No, we do not have enough resources," then there are only two courses of action. First, you can try to obtain more resources. Title 1 and IDEA are funding sources which will let you hire additional interventionists. However, in these days of tight budgets, that may not be possible. The only other option is to "tighten" the requirements so that fewer students are moved into those tiers. This is clearly not ideal, but it is a realistic scenario. You may also find the answer to be, "Yes, we have more than enough resources." If so, you can actually identify *more* students, or you could provide service in smaller groups (perhaps making Tier 2 a three to five student limit, for example).

Using simple numbers, here is an example to estimate the impact on your staffing resources. If a school has 100 students in five first-grade classrooms, there is an average of 20 students per classroom. You can assume that 10 to 20 students will be identified as Tier 1 students after the Universal Screening. This would translate into a single first-grade teacher having to implement intervention for and progress monitor about two to four children. At the end of one or two progress monitoring periods (8 to 16 weeks), you can expect five to ten of the originally identified students to move to Tier 2, which is roughly one to two students per classroom. After 8 to 16 weeks of Tier 2 interventions, you could anticipate one to five of those students to move on to Tier 3. This would translate into one Tier 3 student per classroom, or one student in "every other" classroom. These numbers would be multiplied by four grade-levels and you would have an idea of how many students need the interventionists' time. Again, keep in mind the group sizes available and the time requirements for each tier.

Ultimately, you will need time to ensure that you have the right number of human resources for the number of students being identified. Keep in mind that only in the first year will you have the "first round" of Universal Screening. The first screening will identify new students in every classroom, and all of them will be placed in Tier 1. This will make it *seem* like the interventionists have more free time than they actually will. This burden will even out over time, and there will be students in all three tiers throughout the school year.

Universal Screening—Not the Only Way In

This is a dangerous section to write. The impulse to make exceptions to the rules of a new model can be very, very strong. After all, the model is brand new to your district, and people have questions and doubts. For this reason, we implemented a strict "no exceptions" rule for the first year of our RTI experience. There was great resistance to this, and there was no question that many of the concerns were valid. However, you cannot adjust a system fairly and with integrity until you study the system. Without experience and study, your tweaks are simply attempts to bring a portion of the new program back into your comfort zone. You must resist the urge to tamper with the structure, and you must fight off those who insist you are doing harm.

But there was no question that the Universal Screening mechanism was not perfect. Solely relying on the screening tool to provide students with additional assistance would guarantee that students would "fall through the cracks"—the very cracks that RTI was designed to fill. There are students who might pass the Universal Screening, but who are still at-risk. The type of student who is most often associated with this scenario is the "word-caller." This student is a fluent reader who has trouble comprehending. For this student and others that a classroom teacher has concerns for, a secondary entrance to the tier system was required. We call this system the Request for Review of Records, or R3. With this system, a teacher who has concerns for a student, despite the student's good performance on the Universal Screening, can petition the RTI team to assign the student to Tier 1. The R3 procedures have the teacher gather available information on the student—grades, guided-reading level, Universal Screening scores, past tier placements, standardized test scores, work samples, and so forth—and submit them to the RTI team. The RTI team reviews any R3 submissions at the end of a progress monitoring cycle. If the RTI team agrees, the student is placed in Tier 1 for the next progress monitoring cycle. This is very important because the requesting teachers know that such decisions place the intervention and progress monitoring responsibility directly on them. The R3 process is not about the teacher handing off responsibility for a struggling student, but rather about getting the student into a system where he or she can access necessary resources.

With a Universal Screening tool in place that is efficient, easy to administer, and valid, along with a secondary measure to ensure that all students have access to the RTI resources, the early identification "cracks" are properly sealed. The last "crack" remaining is where the student who never makes enough progress to succeed on his or her own, falls. This leads us to the critical discussion of progress monitoring.

7

What is Progress Monitoring?

There are many aspects of a strong Response to Intervention model that will be very familiar to teachers and other staff. Teachers have been diagnosing potential concerns and intervening on behalf of struggling students since the first schoolhouses were built. On the other hand, using a Universal Screening tool to systematically collect data to identify which students need formal intervention is a new idea to most educators. Another aspect that is foreign to most teachers and school staff is the concept of progress monitoring.

In the RTI system, progress monitoring means regularly collecting data points over a fixed time period to determine the effectiveness of a potentially at-risk student's intervention routine. The monitoring tool should be an extension of the Universal Screening tool. The assessments are called probes, and the probes should adhere to the same criteria that the Universal Screening tool did in terms of efficiency, ease of use, validity, and time. The probes should be easy to administer, take as little time as possible, and have valid results. Some popular progress monitoring tools require just one minute to administer in a one-on-one setting. In elementary school literacy, these probes will rely heavily on oral reading fluency assessments. Students will have a cold read for one minute, and then the educator will count the number of words correctly read with fluency. Over time, this will produce a trend line that the educator can analyze to determine whether or not the student is responding to the intervention. In middle school, comprehension will continue to play a key role in literacy, and foundation skills will be important to learning mathematics. Keep in mind that the goal of the interventions is to address the underlying skill gaps, not just prepare the student for the current content. In a middle school mathematics classroom, a Universal Screen (whether it is an actual assessment or a compilation of data) may identify a student as "at-risk" in math, but it will be critical to diagnose the underlying issues before targeting interventions. An assessment may show that the student scores poorly on data analysis or geometry sections, but the underlying skill gaps may reside in numerical operations, number sense, place value, or other key foundational skills. Teaching a student to use "tricks," mnemonics, or memorization to pass a test will produce short-term results and artificial evidence of gains. Identifying, intervening for, and progress monitoring growth in specific foundational skills will give the student the opportunity to truly understand the content.

Tools

The progress monitoring tool does not need to mirror the Universal Screening tool, but there are many advantages if it does. For example, if a Universal Screening tool and the progress monitoring tool both measure oral reading fluency, then data analysis becomes easier. Educators can note Universal Screening scores on the same graph as progress monitoring data to identify any interesting patterns. Imagine that a student scores poorly on the oral reading fluency portion of the Universal Screen. This student is placed in Tier 1, but then performs above the benchmark consistently during progress monitoring. Clearly this student was inappropriately identified during the screening process. This could happen for a variety of reasons. Perhaps the screener was someone unfamiliar to the student, or maybe the student simply had a bad morning. Regardless, such a student should be removed from the Tier system as soon as it is practical. This would be more difficult if the Universal Screening and progress monitoring tools were different. Consistency of tools also helps in the familiarity for teachers and students. By keeping the variety of tools to a minimum, teachers become more proficient at administering assessments and analyzing the results. The semantics of the tools become a common language among the staff and facilitate an easier exchange of information, both formally and informally. Students will be more comfortable since they are taking an assessment that is consistent in its look and feel. With that comfort comes a greater validity in scores. Most commercial products will have the Universal Screening tool and progress monitoring tool look the same to capitalize on these advantages.

Frequency

Progress monitoring should occur weekly. Each week during the intervention and progress monitoring cycle, a probe or series of probes is given to each student in a Tier. The teacher providing the intervention should administer the progress monitoring probe. In Tier 1, the classroom teacher is responsible, but in Tiers 2 and 3, the interventionist providing instruction is responsible. A progress monitoring cycle should last a minimum of eight weeks. Since school year lengths vary, this cannot be a standardized number for everyone. You should have a minimum of three intervention and progress monitoring cycles during the course of the school year to allow you the flexibility for movement between tiers, as well as make adjustments to interventions. Eight- to ten-week cycles, three to four times a year should fit into everyone's school year. We have used four–eight week cycles successfully in a 40 week school year which allows for Universal Screening time and other interruptions, such as State testing. An eight week cycle is the minimum though, and it does require weekly testing to ensure the collection of a sufficient number of data points.

Data Collection

Data collection should occur weekly during the progress monitoring cycle. This will give the educator enough data points to make accurate decisions regarding the student's response to the intervention. Teachers administering the progress monitoring should take care to have the probes administered in as consistent a manner as possible from week to week. The validity of the probe's data is critical because it assesses the intervention's effectiveness and could provoke intervention changes that then restrict the learning environment more heavily. Administering the probes under the same circumstances during the same day and time each week will add to the validity of the scores. Each week the teacher administering the probes enters the progress monitoring scores into the data collection tool, such as a computer program or website.

Target Line Identified

There are two lines on a progress monitoring graph: the target line and the growth line. The target line is the line connecting the Universal Screening score to the end-of-the year benchmark score. Figures 7.1 and 7.2 on page 48 show the target line. Figure 7.1 displays a target line for a student identified during the first Universal Screening in September. Figure 7.2 shows a target line for a student identified during the second Universal Screening in January. The end-of-the-year benchmark score has been set by the tool creator (e.g., DIBELS or Aimsweb, etc). The slope of this line represents the average rate of growth the student would need to reach the desired benchmark score by the end of the school year.

FIGURE 7.1 Target Line from September Universal Screening

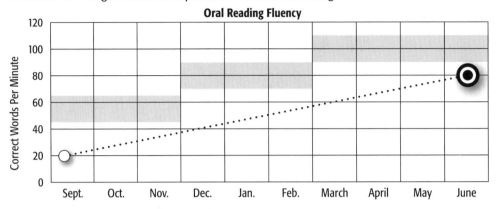

FIGURE 7.2 Target Line from January Universal Screening

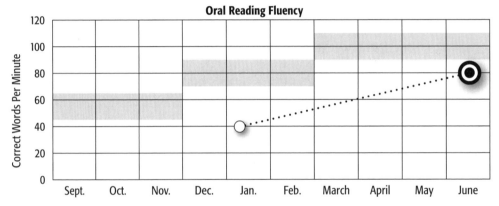

Growth Line Plotted

Data points gathered through progress monitoring are then entered into the software. These points are then plotted on the graph along with the target line. Individual data points are not significant as they only represent single probes. The significance of the data points becomes clear as multiple probe scores are plotted against the target line on the graph. Figures 7.3 and 7.4 represent different versions of figures 7.1 and 7.2. These figures include progress monitoring data points added after eight weeks of intervention.

Response to Intervention Trend Determined

One of the nice things about Response to Intervention is that its acronym represents words that truly mean something. The phrase "response

FIGURE 7.3 Eight-Week Progress-Monitoring Data from September

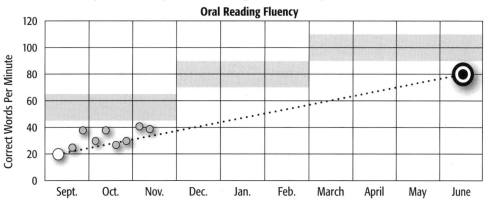

FIGURE 7.4 Eight-Week Progress-Monitoring Data from January

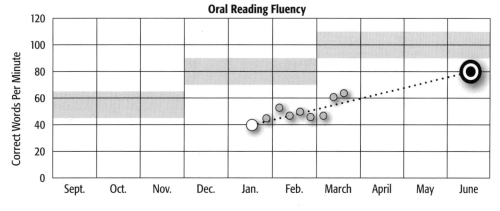

to intervention" refers to how a student is reacting to planned, deliberate attempts to address an identified weakness or to close an identified gap. First we identify a student as potentially at-risk and plan an intervention program to address the identified weaknesses. After eight weeks, we ask the critical RTI question:"How has the student responded to the intervention? This is really the key to the whole program. This is what is really, genuinely different from what we already do. We have always tried to help struggling students. But, so often, those students have been given "help" yet never gotten "better". They receive additional service in the primary grades and they continue to need it for years. Now, with RTI, that cannot happen. Now, we are gathering data to analyze. If the student is not responding to the intervention, we react after only eight weeks rather than years later. Even if that reaction is to "stay the course," we keep track and watch the student closely. The interventions will continue to change and intensify until the child responds positively.

The key determinant is the slope of the growth line. Obviously, the progress monitoring data will not create a nice, straight growth line. However, there will most likely be a trend that presents itself. You can imagine (or literally draw) a line that best represents the trend through the progress monitoring data points. In statistics, this line is called the line of best fit. There are complicated equations to determine the exact line of best fit, but this is not necessary for these purposes. We are not trying to prove something mathematically. We are trying to determine if what we are doing works. This imaginary line has a slope, and the goal is to have that slope be equal to or greater than the target line. We want the student to, at minimum, "hug" the target line. If they do, they will reach the benchmark by the end of the year and have successfully closed the gap that the Universal Screening tool identified. If the slope of the growth line is greater than the target line, the gap is closing. If the slope is less, the gap is widening. Some discussions at the RTI team meetings will certainly be more complicated than this, but there will be many discussions that simply state, "The gap is closing, let's keep doing what we are doing," which would leave the student in the tier he or she is already in.

The Power of the Visual

It was an enlightening moment when we first started printing progress monitoring graphs for students. These two vignettes catch the essence of the power that a data-backed visual brought to our efforts.

The Teacher—Buddy had been diagnosed as "needing intensive intervention" by the Universal Screening tool in September. This was the first year of RTI, and Mrs. Karigan had begun her "official" Tier 1 interventions with Buddy, which consisted of working with him one-on-one for 10 minutes daily after lunch, pairing him up with a friend for a specific task three times a week while she led a guided reading group, and giving him a specialized center to work at during center time. These were all efforts she may have made anyway for Buddy, but her attention was heightened by the new RTI system. After five weeks of intervention, Mrs. Karigan decided to print out Buddy's progress monitoring report. Even though the eight-week cycle was not yet over, she was curious about the effects her efforts had on Buddy, and how this RTI program would communicate them to her. The graph showed Buddy's growth line slope rising much faster than the target line! At this rate, he would be on grade level by December! Mrs. Karigan literally ran down the hallway with Buddy's graph and told anyone who would listen, "It's working! It's working!"

Surely, this teacher knew why she was helping her student, and probably had great confidence that her efforts were effective. But the visual, this concrete statement that the decisions she was making and the strategies she was employing were working, affirmed and further motivated her.

The Parent—Megan had been assessed as "needing intensive intervention" by the Universal Screening in September. Among other issues that the teacher saw (and the Universal Screening confirmed) was that Megan struggled with basic letter recognition. The teacher would certainly work on this, but this was an area where the parent could provide a great deal of reinforcement. The teacher held a brief conference with Megan's mom to go over the Universal Screening results, discuss what "Tier 1" meant, and ask for her help with Megan's letter recognition. The teacher gave Megan's mom a bag of magnetic letters and told her to put them on the refrigerator door at home. She asked Megan's mother to challenge her daughter to name a letter every time she passed the refrigerator and, if she was correct, she could move it to the freezer side. Megan's mom took the bag home and did what was asked. In the next few weeks, she wrote at note to the teacher saying that Megan would start going to the kitchen for no other reason than to hold up a letter, name it, and move it to the other side. Her mom would sometimes have to help or correct Megan, but Megan stayed interested. Four weeks later, the teacher asked Megan's mom to come in for a quick conference to show her something. The teacher had printed out the progress monitoring graph for letter recognition showing Megan's growth line leaping off the chart. She told Megan's mother that, because of her efforts, her daughter was no longer considered a Tier 1 student for letter recognition. Her mom's response? "What else can I do!?"

How desperately would you like a parent to look to you and ask, "What can I do?" and really mean it? This mom is going to do all the teacher asks because she has seen—on paper, with data—the results of her efforts. This is motivating and affirming, and has secured an active, interested parent for the rest of the school year.

More on Middle School and Progress Monitoring

We mentioned above that there are several reasons that having a similar progress monitoring tool and Universal Screening tool is advantageous. However, we also said that a Universal Screening at the middle school level may be unnecessary considering the amount of data that has already been collected. If you choose to use a rubric or compilation of data to identify students as "at-risk," there is nothing to model your progress monitoring tool after. In addition, if you use a compilation of data, you also do not have a diagnostic tool that helps identify the foundation skill gaps. We suggest that, once a student has been identified through a compilation of data system, you use a diagnostic tool to help identify underlying concerns. These concerns would be the focus of the intervention, and can then be progress monitored. For example, a student received a "D" in 6th grade math and failed to reach proficiency on the state standardized test. Let's say that your rubric calls for that student to be placed in Tier 1 at the beginning of 7th grade. Those two pieces of information have helped identify the student as "at-risk." but they provide us little helpful information when it comes time for intervention planning. Before interventions begin, the student should be given a diagnostic assessment. This diagnostic may reveal a weakness in number sense and a lack of understanding of place value when using decimals. Those skills become the targets of the interventions and the progress monitoring tool should be directly related to them. As those skills improve, we would expect overall performance to improve.

Progress monitoring is as key to the RTI model as any other single component. It is, along with Universal Screening, the link to data-based decision making. It is a critical component to determining adequate response to intervention and, therefore, it is key to ensuring that any "cracks" that students might fall through are permanently sealed.

8

Who is the RTI Team and What Do They Do?

At various times of the RTI process, a small group of building-based educators who make up the RTI team make decisions regarding the tier placement and movement of students through the system. The RTI team meets on a regular basis throughout the school year. Its primary purpose is to review progress monitoring data about each student that is in an RTI tier, and then determines his or her placement for the next intervention cycle. Note the meeting times for the RTI team on the sample RTI calendar in Figure 8.1 on page 54.

The RTI team meets at the end of each Intervention cycle (called progress monitoring #1–#4 on the calendar). As you can see, the team meets after each eight-week cycle when students have been progress monitored. It doesn't matter what tier or grade the students are in, these cycles remain constant throughout the school. Their primary purposes are 1) to determine whether or not the student is responding to the interventions provided over the eight weeks, and 2) to determine that student's tier placement for the next eight-week cycle. Thus, the RTI team becomes the "gatekeeper" of the tier movement process.

RTI Team Members

Each school has one RTI team with three permanent members and one rotating member. The three permanent members are a building administrator, a Reading Specialist, and a Child Study Team member. The fourth member is a classroom teacher who represents the grade level that is being discussed. This fourth member will rotate depending on the grade level of

FIGURE 8.1 Response to Intervention Calendar

Week #	Week of	School-wide Actions	Teacher, RTI team, CST Actions
1	7-Sep		
2	14-Sep	Begin Universal Screening (US) #1	Students identified for Tier One interventions
3	21-Sep	Scores entered for US #1	
4	28-Sep	Progress monitoring begins	Weekly progress monitoring data submitted to CST Liaison for any Tier Three student
5	5-Oct		
6	12-Oct		
7	19-Oct		
8	26-Oct		
9	2-Nov		
10	9-Nov		
11	16-Nov	Progress monitoring #1 ends	Progress monitoring reports submitted to RTI team
12	23-Nov	RTI team meets	Review PM data and determine if adequate RTI is noted—determine tier changes
13	30-Nov	Progress monitoring #2 begins	Weekly progress monitoring data submitted to CST Liaison for any Tier Three student
14	7-Dec		
15	14-Dec		
16	21-Dec		
17	28-Dec	School Closed	
18	4-Jan	Progress monitoring #2 cont.	
19	11-Jan		
20	18-Jan		
21	25-Jan	Begin Universal Screening #2	
22	1-Feb	Scores entered US #2 Progress monitoring #2 ends	Students identified for Tier One interventions Progress monitoring reports submitted to RTI team
23	8-Feb	RTI team meets	Review PM data and determine if adequate RTI is noted—determine tier changes

FIGURE 8.1 Response to Intervention Calendar *(continued)*

Week #	Week of	School-wide Actions	Teacher, RTI team, CST Actions
24	15-Feb	Progress monitoring #3 begins	Weekly progress monitoring data submitted to CST Liaison for any Tier Three student
25	22-Feb		
26	1-Mar		
27	8-Mar		
28	15-Mar		
29	22-Mar		
30	29-Mar		
31	5-Apr	Progress monitoring #3 ends	Progress monitoring reports submitted to RTI team
32	12-Apr	RTI team meets	Review PM data and determine if adequate RTI is noted—determine tier changes
33	19-Apr	Progress monitoring #4 begins	
34	26-Apr		
35	3-May	Begin Universal Screening #3	
36	10-May	Scores entered US #3	Growth information available for all students
37	17-May		
38	24-May	Progress monitoring #4 ends	Progress monitoring reports submitted to RTI team
39	31-May	RTI team meets to place for 10-11	Review PM data and determine Tier assignments for September 2010

students being discussed at that meeting. Most districts and schools have a Student Study Team, Intervention and Referral Services (I&RS) team, Student Intervention Team, or another title that represents a group of individuals who discuss strategies to assist a struggling student. The make-up of these teams reflects a desire to have a variety of viewpoints when addressing a student's concerns. The design of the RTI team is similar. The building administrator is on the team to offer a global perspective and to ensure that the proper RTI procedures are followed. The Reading Specialist brings critical knowledge of the curriculum, expertise in available interventions that have been used in the past, and specialized knowledge of how students acquire language and reading skills. Having a Child Study Team representative has several benefits. First, the representative brings knowledge of learning disabilities, as well as experience with struggling students. Second, he or she has a more global perspective on the range of challenges that students face, which the classroom teacher may not have. Third, the representative's presence ensures that the Child Study Team knows about any student moving through the RTI system. This contributes to the "seamless integration" of general education and special education that RTI promotes. Having a grade-level classroom teacher as another representative ensures the voice of the classroom teacher is heard and brings the knowledge of the classroom expectations to the table. Keeping this team small allows for it to move efficiently through the process.

Data Collected for Meetings

The RTI team's purpose is to review the data concerning students who are in an RTI system tier. There are two primary sources of data that the classroom teacher supplements with other data. The first is the progress monitoring graph. As discussed in chapter 7, the progress monitoring graph compares the student's progress over time to a target growth line that represents minimum grade-level competency. The second primary source of data is the Student Intervention Tracking form. As discussed in the next chapter, this form documents data that is critical to analyzing the intervention's effectiveness. The form documents the type, frequency, and duration of each intervention; the group size during the intervention, and anecdotal notes from the teacher. The classroom teacher may present additional data for the team's consideration. Such data may include writing samples, running records, information regarding guided reading level growth, or other student work.

The RTI Meeting

The RTI Team is entrusted with the important job of directing struggling students' future tier movements. The RTI meeting's main objective is to determine if each student is responding adequately to intervention. Team members are asked to look objectively at all of the data presented and to decide on a course of action based on the trends they are able to see.

The first piece of important data is the Student Intervention Tracking form filled out by the teacher providing the intervention for the student. This form is vital because it provides the teacher with a voice at the meeting. The team needs to decide if the interventions were implemented with fidelity. The

FIGURE 8.2 Target Line Development

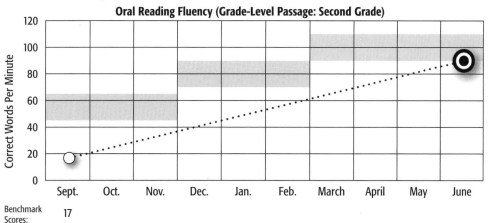

Benchmark Scores: 17

team examines information regarding the intervention used, the frequency of its use, the size of the intervention group, and the duration of the intervention to determine if they were carried out as originally intended. If they were, the team will move on to the progress monitoring graphs. If the interventions were not given with the intended fidelity, the team suggests ways to strengthen the intervention, and the student may remain in his or her current tier for another eight-week cycle. This form allows the RTI Team to encourage all teachers to put the necessary effort into the interventions. Not doing so alters the progress monitoring data immensely.

Once the team begins to look at the progress monitoring graphs, they will be utilizing the "slope rule." The progress monitoring chart in Figure 8.2 plots a dotted aim line from where the student started at the Universal Screening to the desired target for the end of the year. This target is placed at the minimum level of proficiency for a grade-level student at that time of year. The aim line shows the rate of growth that the student must demonstrate in order to reach that target.

The small circles in the second graph represent the progress monitoring probes. If the line of best fit for the progress monitoring probes has a slope equal to or greater than the aim line, the child is making adequate progress. The child is showing enough response to the interventions that it appears as if he or she will reach the target by year's end. If the slope of the line of best fit is less than that of the aim line, the student is not projected to reach the target by year's end and the intervention should be altered. In Figure 8.3, the line of best fit appears to be greater than the aim line, and thus the student should continue with the interventions.

While the "slope rule" does not have a formula attached to it, the RTI team can make informed decisions when combining the data from the progress

FIGURE 8.3 Line of Best Fit

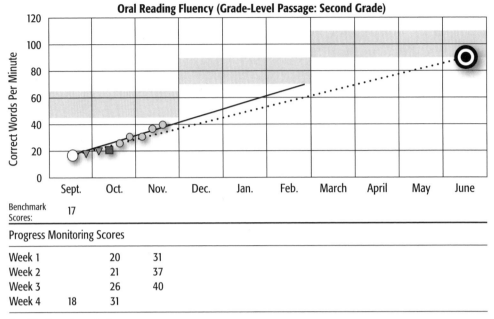

Benchmark Scores: 17

Progress Monitoring Scores

Week 1		20	31
Week 2		21	37
Week 3		26	40
Week 4	18	31	

Key: ◯ = At or above aim line
▽ = Below aim line
◼ = Consider adjusting intervention (within current tier)

monitoring graphs with the information from the Student Intervention Tracking form. While doing this, the team must always focus on student growth instead of comparing student work to a grade-level benchmark. Struggling students who are receiving supplementary instruction probably have difficulty with the grade-level assignments they are given in the classroom. It is very easy to look at the student's frustration with this difficulty and say that the intervention is not working. "If the student is unable to do the grade-level work, we must try something else," is a common mantra of classroom personnel and parents. The RTI team must look past this idea to focus on the growth that the student is or is not showing. There are many times when the student being discussed will have an adequate response to the intervention, but will still struggle in the classroom. In Figure 8.4, the slope of the progress monitoring data points exceeds the aim line, thus the student is showing an adequate response to the intervention. Notice however that the student's progress monitoring data points are still well below the gray, shaded bar that represents the average grade-level achievement. This student is responding well to the interventions and should reach the target by the end of the school year. The problem is that, at the present time, grade-level work is still too difficult for the student. The RTI Team must place more weight on

FIGURE 8.4 Student Growth vs. Grade Level Expectations

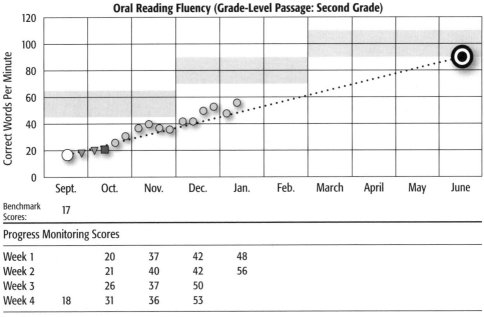

Benchmark Scores:	17				

Progress Monitoring Scores

Week 1		20	37	42	48
Week 2		21	40	42	56
Week 3		26	37	50	
Week 4	18	31	36	53	

the student's growth and trust that the intervention will lead the student to success.

Conversely, a positive slope of the progress monitoring data may not always represent adequate response to intervention. As demonstrated in Figure 8.5 on page 60, the line of best fit of the progress monitoring data shows a positive trend. However, the slope of that line is less than the aim line, resulting in an increasing gap between actual progress and required progress. This is not an adequate response to intervention and would require action on the part of the RTI team.

It is important for the RTI team to recognize that the progress monitoring data does not always reflect purely academic issues. Figure 8.6 on page 61 illustrates the performance of a student who was showing adequate response to the interventions and then, seemingly without explanation, began to perform erratically. There is no academic reason for a student to switch from being able to consistently read over 60 words per minute to not being able to do so for three straight weeks. The RTI team should not make a tier movement determination without further investigation. There may have been an emotional event in this child's life or some social impact within the classroom. Perhaps the primary teacher has just left on a medical leave, perhaps there has been a death in the family, or perhaps there was simply a fight with friends. When faced with such data, the RTI team should gather more information before intensifying an academic intervention.

FIGURE 8.5 Positive Growth vs. Adequate Response

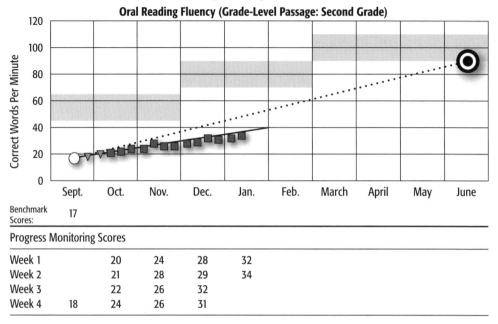

Oral Reading Fluency (Grade-Level Passage: Second Grade)

Benchmark Scores:	17			

Progress Monitoring Scores

Week 1		20	24	28	32
Week 2		21	28	29	34
Week 3		22	26	32	
Week 4	18	24	26	31	

RTI Team Decisions

There are three possible options for each student discussed at the RTI meeting. Decisions about a student's intervention are made based on the available data and will remain in place for that student over the next eight-week progress monitoring cycle.

One option is to leave the student in his or her current tier. This is appropriate for many students who are showing adequate response to intervention. It is not realistic to assume that students will be ready for less intensive interventions after a mere eight-week cycle. It is also not appropriate to assume that every student needs to move to a more intensive tier to "speed up" the rate of growth. Quality remediation takes time and it is important to provide students in tiers with enough of it. While there is no steadfast rule that requires students to spend more than one cycle in a tier, it is assumed that many students will. It is also appropriate for the RTI team to recommend changes in the intervention without changes in the tier. Should the RTI team members feel that the student would benefit from modifications to the current intervention, they should make these recommendations to the teacher through the Reading Specialist and grade-level representative.

Another potential decision would be to move a student to a less intensive tier. The advantage of this is multi-faceted. First, moving a student to a less intensive tier frees up the interventionist's time. If a student moves from Tier 3 to Tier 2, the interventionist seeing that child goes from seeing the child

FIGURE 8.6 Looking at the Whole Child

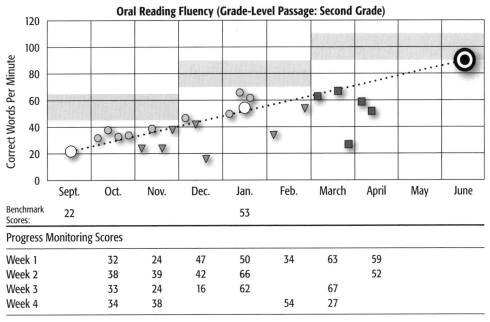

Progress Monitoring Scores							
Week 1	32	24	47	50	34	63	59
Week 2	38	39	42	66			52
Week 3	33	24	16	62		67	
Week 4	34	38			54	27	

in a group of one or two students for 45 to 60 minutes to seeing that child in a group of four to six for 30 to 45 minutes. Second, moving to a less intensive tier still lets the interventionist progress monitor the student. If there is any change in the student's response to the new interventions, the team will pick it up during the next cycle. Finally, a basic tenet of RTI philosophy is to provide interventions in the least restrictive environment possible. Moving a child back a tier should be celebrated as a true victory on the part of the student and the interventionist.

Moving a student to a more intensive tier is a third option available to the RTI Team. If a student does not show adequate response to intervention and the interventions have already been modified, it may be time to change the intensity of the intervention. Moving to a more intensive tier often changes who is providing the intervention service or changes the intervention's frequency and duration. Both of these changes are legitimate options if a student shows a lack of response to intervention.

The final option for an RTI team is to remove a student from the tier structure completely. This is only an option for students who are in Tier 1 and you should only consider it when the progress monitoring graph securely places the child in the shaded gray bar that indicates grade-level proficiency. While this certainly should be celebrated as a victory for the student, it is important to remember that a student is no longer progress monitored after he or she leaves the tier structure. The student would not be assessed again until the next Universal Screening occurs.

Fidelity of the RTI Team

While the importance of the fidelity of the interventions has been discussed at length, the fidelity of the decisions made by the RTI team is of equal importance. A building administrator or another lead person must look at trends within the tier movement data between classes and, in a multi-school system, between schools.

A school should collect data about tier movement at each grade level. Is one grade level consistently moving students through the tiers in rapid succession? Is there a grade level that seems to achieve more success when it keeps students in the tier system for more than one cycle? Do students have an equal chance at moving back to a less intensive tier as they do moving to a more intensive tier? The answers to these questions allow building-level leaders to ensure that all students have the same access to intervention. The answers also force the RTI team to look carefully at the fidelity of intervention forms, and at their own practices and decisions. Opportunities to look at data allow educators to make informed decisions about what is really happening within their school, as opposed to simply relying on a feeling. Tier Movement Tracking forms provide this assistance in an RTI model.

It is also important to monitor this data across schools in a district where more than one school is implementing an RTI model. Again, the issue comes down to one of equity. Every student in a district should have equal access to interventions in the least restrictive environment possible. If teams in different schools operate under different assumptions, this will not happen. RTI teams need to be on the same page when it comes to application of the "slope rule" and determining the fidelity of interventions. RTI's core beliefs must guide everyone involved, thus creating the best environment for similar meetings to occur regardless of building.

RTI Team vs. Other Student Improvement Teams

When a district starts a Response to Intervention initiative, it is usually in addition to an already established Student Improvement team. Many of these teams are mandated by government agencies and have varying degrees of success. Regardless of the formal name (Student Study Team, Pupil Assistance Committee, Intervention and Referral Services Team, or other), these groups are generally comprised of various educators who come together for the express purpose of suggesting intervention for the struggling student. The struggles may be academic or behavioral in nature, and vary widely in intensity. These committees often include many professionals from outside the classroom including the school nurse, a guidance counselor, a speech therapist, a Child Study Team member, and other similar staff members. These teams can continue to exist with an RTI structure in place. In the model outlined in this text, the RTI team is responsible for all decisions relating to academic areas that are Universally Screened and progress monitored. Without a quality Universal Screening or progress monitoring tool, an RTI structure cannot exist. This requirement makes it difficult for the RTI team to make judgments in some subject areas. The Student Improvement Team still makes decisions for other academic areas, as well as for behavior and non-academic issues.

As noted many times before, the model outlined in this text focuses heavily on language arts literacy development. The proponents of this model designed it in this manner because of the heavy research base supporting the use of DIBELS as a legitimate means of predicting future literacy success. In order for a Universal Screening tool to be effective it needs to diagnose, not report achievement. If you cannot find a good tool, then the existing Student Improvement Team would have to assist the teacher in finding interventions. If a district wants to have a true RTI model in place, the foundation needs to be in a research-based Universal Screening and progress monitoring tool.

However, these existing Student Improvement Teams should go through a transformation. The RTI core beliefs seep into the mannerisms of the Student Improvement Team even though they are not officially bound by the tier structure. When they are not trying to provide assistance in the least restrictive environment possible, teachers and administrators on these teams are asked to continually intensify the interventions provided. The difference is that there is no formal tier structure and teachers are not progress monitoring the interventions.

The RTI team is an integral part of the school's culture. While it is officially the "gate-keeper" of tier movement for academic interventions, the core beliefs of the RTI structure bleed into all areas that provide intervention. This team is held in high esteem in the building, and it performs vital services for struggling students. Our attention now turns to what happens in the tiers that the RTI team assigns.

9

What Happens in Tier 1?

As we have mentioned before, many Response to Intervention models view a strong core curriculum as a universal Tier 1 in which all students are a part of the intervention and progress monitoring process. We submit that a strong core curriculum and differentiated instruction in the classroom are essential components of any school, regardless of an RTI system. The existence of a strong core curriculum (along with the professional development that is essential to deliver it) coupled with daily, planned, differentiated instruction provides the necessary foundation for quality education. The term "progress monitoring" is not unique to Response to Intervention. Formal assessments such as benchmark assessments, chapter tests, and the "Friday spelling test" are all forms of progress monitoring in the traditional classroom. Informal assessments such as daily edits, quick quizzes, and general teacher observation are also forms of progress monitoring. Think of the best teachers you know. They informally and formally assess their students on a regular basis, know where each of their students is and what they need to accomplish next. They ask more of the students who are ready to accomplish more and alter instruction to best meet the needs of their struggling students. They don't need to call their classroom "Tier 1" to do this. This type of teacher, with a strong curriculum to support them, creates the quality classroom experience we want for all students. This is a goal outside of an RTI system. The RTI system is designed to complement that classroom, thus providing structure and resources for the student who needs more support. As these students are identified, they are placed in Tier 1.

What Happens in Tier 1

When a student is placed in Tier 1, they are to receive deliberate, planned interventions to encourage growth in areas identified as concerns. The teacher provides these interventions are during the course of the regular school day. To an outside observer, these interventions are no different than the help any child who is having difficulty would receive. The difference is that these students have been formally identified by the screening tool, will participate in intentionally planned, research-based activities, and their progress will be formally monitored over a period of eight weeks.

Tier 1 Doesn't Come in a Kit

Despite what many publishing companies would like for you to think, Tier 1 doesn't come in a kit. Once you have decided to "do" Response to Intervention, the natural tendency of educators is to look for the packaged product that will support the effort. There will be many offerings labeled "Supports Response to Intervention" and "Pyramid of Interventions Compatible" at the tables in the vendor areas of any convention. These products are very tempting, but there is no shortcut to a great RTI program. The road to a great RTI program is paved with a commitment to research-based instructional strategies and strong professional development. Again, think of the best teachers you know. Are they the best teachers because they have the most complete boxed sets of materials? No. It is because they can quickly diagnose and expertly intervene with a student. You can't buy that from a vendor. Fortunately, most schools already have such expertise at their disposal.

One early challenge of getting a Response to Intervention program running in your school or district is convincing teachers that Tier 1 interventions already occur in their classrooms. This becomes one of those messages that must be continually "preached" to staff. Tier 1 interventions are already happening, RTI just adds more structure, provides tools for standardizing progress monitoring, and ensures that ineffective intervention does not continue unchecked. Teachers know early on in every school year who among their students are struggling. Once the students are recognized, teachers will intervene to address those students' specific identified needs. Such interventions include small group instruction, extra attention from the teacher, differentiated questioning, differentiated centers, deliberate "buddy" selection for paired activities, and deliberate selection of activities for independent work. Teachers routinely do this at every grade level and in every subject. What they haven't realized is that this is what Tier 1 is all about: early identification and immediate intervention for any struggling student. Imagine this vignette prior to an RTI structure being introduced to the school.

> Mrs. Perez is a first grade teacher with 24 students in her class. Through observation and informal record keeping, she notices that Maria and Peter are having difficulty with some reading activities. Mrs. Perez takes them aside during center time and has each do a quick read for her as she takes a running record. She quickly recognizes that Maria is having difficulty with initial sound identification and Peter still cannot identify certain letters. Over the next few days, Mrs. Perez uses this information in several ways. In class, she deliberately chooses centers that are appropriate for the skill levels of each child and that address their individual needs. Mrs. Perez contacts Maria's parents for a quick conference. At the conference, Mrs. Perez gives the parents "initial sound boxes," which contain items that all start with the same letter and also contain a set of cards with the items' names written on them. She describes to the parents how to use the boxes with Maria. Back in class, Mrs. Perez matches Peter with Gabriella, a stronger student with some social interaction concerns, to a letter identification game during paired activity time. Gabriella benefits from the social interaction and Peter works with his letters. During morning message time, Mrs. Perez deliberately calls on Maria to identify the beginning sounds of words, and she calls on Peter to identify letters that he struggles with. Over the next few weeks, Mrs. Perez pays close attention to the progress that Maria is making with her initial sound fluency, and also keeps track of Peter's letter identification progress.

This is not a story that would stand out as unusual in most schools. Most teachers implement these types of activities every day. What Mrs. Perez is doing is at the core of the Response to Intervention philosophy. She has identified concerns early, intervened with appropriate activities, and monitored her students' progress to see if she needs to continue, or try other interventions. With this intervention format, this could just as easily be a story about Ms. Johnson and her 6th grade pre-algebra class. So, if this is the norm, what does RTI do for Mrs. Perez? Let us consider the same vignette in a school with a strong Response to Intervention system in place.

> Mrs. Perez is a first grade teacher with 24 students in her class. Her students have taken the Universal Screening assessment and she has two students, Maria and Peter, who have been identified as "potentially at-risk" and placed in Tier 1 in the RTI system. Mrs. Perez takes them aside during center time and has each do a quick read for her as she takes a running record. She quickly confirms that Maria is having difficulty with initial sound identification, and Peter still has letters that he cannot identify. Over the next few days,

Mrs. Perez uses this information in several ways. In class, she deliberately chooses centers that are appropriate for the skill levels of each child and which address their individual needs. Mrs. Perez contacts Maria's parents for a quick conference. At the conference, Mrs. Perez gives the parents "initial sound boxes," which contain items that all start with the same letter and also contain a set of cards with the items' names written on them. She describes how to use the boxes with Maria. Back in class, Mrs. Perez matches Peter with Gabriella, a stronger student with some social interaction concerns, to a letter identification game during paired activity time. Gabriella benefits from the social interaction, and Peter works with his letters. During morning message time, Mrs. Perez deliberately calls on Maria to identify the beginning sounds of words, and she calls on Peter to identify letters that he is struggling with. She records all of the extra efforts directed specifically at these two students on her RTI intervention sheet.

Each week for the next few weeks, Mrs. Perez gives short progress monitoring probes to both children and records the results. After four weeks, Mrs. Perez notices that Peter has made tremendous progress and knows nearly all of his letters. After the same four weeks, Mrs. Perez also notices that Maria still struggles with her initial sounds. Having noticed that Maria squints when she reads, Mrs. Perez asks the school nurse to check Maria's eyesight, just in case. She will also adjust the amount of time she spends with Maria and gives her some more individual attention. After eight weeks, Mrs. Perez submits the progress monitoring information and her RTI intervention records to the school RTI team. The team determines that Peter has responded adequately to the interventions that Mrs. Perez put in place, and so they remove him from the Tier system. The information suggests that Maria has begun to make some progress, but not enough. The team recommends keeping Maria in Tier 1 for another eight weeks. If she does not show an adequate response to intervention in another eight weeks, she will be moved to Tier 2 and given additional support outside of the classroom.

This vignette illustrates that Tier 1 interventions already exist in good classrooms in your school, but that the process of an RTI system provides a structure that both supports the teacher and ensures effective interventions for the student. The Universal Screening and the subsequent placing of a student "officially" into an RTI tier promotes a sense of urgency and directs focused attention on a problem. It raises the awareness level of the teacher, and provides insurance that this concern will not be overlooked or reduced in priority. The recording of interventions and the submission of progress monitoring scores keeps the teacher accountable and adds another level of insurance that the interventions take place on a regular basis. The progress monitoring scores provide immediate feedback, which allows the teacher to react quickly. Notice that Mrs. Perez did not wait for eight weeks to pass before realizing that Maria was not progressing at the rate she would like. Additionally, Mrs. Perez decided to include another professional (the nurse) and increase her level of intervention in the classroom. She also was able to see that her interventions for Peter were effective and necessitated no changes. Maria will continue to receive increasingly intensive interventions until the teacher finds the degree, type, and frequency that Maria needs.

Creating Your Own Tier 1 "Kit"

Certainly not every teacher is like Mrs. Perez. Many are close, but do not even realize it. These teachers will still be on the lookout for the Tier 1 Kit. They will seek the published product that promises to tell you what single activity to do to address any and all concerns. Again, many publishers will be glad to sell you such a product. However, such products take away the best resource that you have at your disposal: the accumulated experience and expertise of your staff. Instead of buying products, we suggest that you corral that experience and expertise to create your own Tier 1 kit. This will have several positive results. First, as teachers participate in this exercise they will have a greater feeling of involvement and investment in the process. Second, they will feel that they have resources to turn to when students in their classrooms are placed in Tier 1. Third, after realizing that they and their colleagues have accumulated such resources over the years, they will be much more willing to take risks to create and apply new strategies and ideas to their students' learning experiences.

The procedure for this is actually quite simple and yet very effective. Bring your staff together for a faculty meeting or during an in-service. If you have a large enough staff, bring teachers together by grade level. If that would leave less than ten teachers in a group, then you can group kindergarten and first grade together, second and third grade together, and so on. In a middle school setting, you would group teachers by subject area as well as grade. Once in their groups, provide them with recording paper that looks like the example in Figure 9.1 on page 70.

Have teachers pair up and record the first identified concern. For the younger grades, the concerns may be letter identification or beginning sound fluency. For other grades it may be medial sound fluency or oral fluency. For middle school grades, it will be subject area specific. For this example, we will use beginning sound fluency. Direct teachers to have one member of each pair write "Beginning Sound Fluency" in the blank next to "Identified Concern." Next, tell the teachers that they will have three minutes to discuss

FIGURE 9.1 Creating Your Own Tier 1 "Kit"

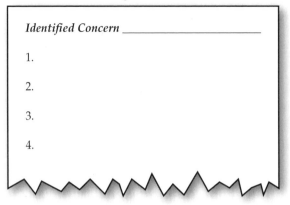

the following question and record all of their answers. The question is: What do you do for a student when you recognize that he or she has difficulty with beginning sound fluency? Have teachers write down everything that their pair says. After three minutes, rotate to different pairs and ask a different question. You can return to the questions more than once since teachers will be with different partners, and this may spark different responses. At the end of the exercise, collect the papers and have them recorded neatly for later distribution. You now have your kit: The collected knowledge of dozens of your teachers, representing decades of experience in creating and implementing hundreds of activities, is now recorded for their reference. This seems like a very simple exercise, and it is. It is also very effective.

Ensuring Intervention Fidelity

As with any system in any industry, an effective RTI system relies on fidelity of implementation. There are several areas where being true to the core RTI beliefs are absolutely critical. The intervention's delivery is certainly one of those areas.

In the business world, fidelity of implementation is more often referred to as "quality control". Companies implement specific processes and protocols to ensure that procedures are followed as designed. The RTI system needs such processes and protocols as well. Imagine a system that identifies struggling students through a Universal Screening tool, classifies those students as needing intervention, and then labels them "Tier 1," only to have that student receive little or no extra help. When an identified student's information is brought to the RTI team, he or she would show little progress, which would

FIGURE 9.2 Sample Intervention Reporting Form

Intervention Used	Length of Time	Frequency	Group Size	Comments
Pair activity—Letter identification game	20 minutes	Every other day	2	Enjoys working with a peer, improvement shown in PM

lead the RTI team to recommend the student for more intensive interventions in Tier 2. Without ensuring that interventions are faithfully and determinedly implemented in the classroom, the RTI system runs the great risk of wasting the student's precious time, having that the student fall further behind the grade-level expectations, putting the student in a more restrictive environment without cause and, potentially, diagnosing a learning disability where none exists. "Quality control" is essential in an RTI system.

The quality control of Tier 1 comes through documentation of interventions. Classroom teachers are required to submit a summary of the interventions employed to the RTI team at the end of the eight week progress monitoring period. The documentation is a simple process as the sample Intervention form in Figure 9.2 illustrates.

The information required is very straightforward. During the eight weeks, the teacher records the interventions used, the length of time that the intervention was used, the frequency of the intervention during each week, and the size of the group participating in the intervention. For example, Mrs. Perez (from our earlier vignette) would record the following on Peter's intervention form, which we have shown in Figure 9.3 on page 72.

This information will be very useful to the RTI team. Assuming several other interventions are also listed, it shows that Mrs. Perez is deliberately planning activities to address Peter's specific concerns, and is taking note on the success of those efforts. From a "quality control" standpoint, Mrs. Perez knows that the RTI team will look for legitimate, well-designed interventions to be in place. She knows that the RTI team will critically evaluate whether enough is done in Tier 1 before deciding to move a student to Tier 2. There is a powerful accountability component when a teacher must record his or her efforts and submit them to a team that will make decisions regarding a student's needs.

In addition to the accountability power of the intervention form, the form also provides a great opportunity for collaboration and intervention improvement.

FIGURE 9.3 Blank Intervention Reporting Form

Progress-Monitoring Week	Intervention Used	Length of Time	Frequency	Group Size	Comments
1					
2					
3					

10

What Happens If In-Class Interventions Aren't Enough?

The essence of a good RTI system is that it reacts quickly and decisively when students continue to struggle despite genuine, sound efforts on the part of the school personnel. A good RTI system forever takes out of the vocabulary the phrases that a student "fell through the cracks" or "was pushed through." With the use of a Universal Screening tool that identifies students early followed by Tier 1 interventions that are introduced immediately afterwards, the next step is to ensure that additional resources are available should the Tier 1 interventions fail to achieve the desired results. Students who do not show adequate responses to Tier 1 interventions would be moved into Tier 2.

How Does a Student Get Into Tier 2?

There is only one way for a student to get into Tier 2: when the RTI team determines that the student is not responding adequately to interventions that have been faithfully implemented for a reasonable amount of time. This is a critical point to keep revisiting. If students are moved into tiers with greater intensity of intervention and more restrictive environments without following the protocols laid out in chapter 5, then the RTI structure has failed. The pillars of an RTI system—data-driven decisions, creation of the least restrictive environment possible, progressively increasing intensity of interventions, progress monitoring to assess effectiveness—will all have been abandoned. This is so critical since a lack of data-driven decisions, an absence of criteria that distributes resources, inconsistency in determining what interventions are needed, and disagreement on what constitutes adequate response to an intervention cause many current systems to fail. So, to reiterate, **there is only one way into Tier 2** and that is an inadequate response to the Tier 1 interventions as determined by the RTI team.

Any bold and underlined rule should have an exception, and this one is no different. Yes, there is another way into Tier 2 besides the "only way" rule noted above, but it is not a "loophole". It is just an exception based on good information. A student moving into the district with documented interventions from their previous school can be moved into the tier that has the corresponding interventions. This is a good idea for a few reasons, and there are several safeguards to ensure the integrity of the RTI system. This is a good idea because you do not want to provide less service than the level mandated by other educational professionals. If a student moves into your school with documentation of an intensive intervention, such as *Reading Recovery*, it would be irresponsible to make that child wait for a Universal Screening and then place him or her into Tier 1 interventions. That child should be immediately placed in Tier 3. Other students may arrive with documentation of supplemental pull-out sessions with a specialist. It would be appropriate to place these students in a Tier 2 setting. In such cases, safeguards to prevent "over-intervening" exist within the RTI structure. Once an interventionist begins progress monitoring, the student's abilities will be ascertained quickly. If the assigned tier was too intensive, the RTI team can move the student back into a less restrictive tier. Also, there is always another Universal Screening within a few weeks or months, depending on when the child moves into the district. After the Universal Screening, the RTI process should take over. If the new student was placed in Tier 2 and passes the Universal Screening, the child should be removed from the tier system altogether.

What are Tier 2 Interventions?

The purpose of moving a student to Tier 2 is to intensify the intervention in the case of an absent or an inadequate response to Tier 1 interventions. Tier 2 interventions supplement classroom instruction and take place outside of the regular classroom instructional block. This usually happens physically outside of the classroom, as students are brought to a small group instruction area with minimal distractions. It is important to note that a change in tier means a change in *intensity* of intervention, not just a change in physical location.

Most schools have staff members who do not have primary classroom responsibilities. Instead, they are specifically charged with assisting struggling

FIGURE 10.1 Tier 2 Guidelines

Frequency	Duration	Number of Students
3 times a week or "every other day"	Minimum of 30 minutes	4 to 6 students

children. Some schools have Reading Specialists or basic skills instructors, or sometimes both. These teachers are the primary staff members who deliver Tier 2 interventions. Special Education teachers can also deliver Tier 2 interventions, if their schedules allow.

Tier 2 interventions will remove a student from his or her classroom to meet with a small group of students and a teacher. Guidelines for the frequency, duration, and group size for Tier 2 interventions are summarized in Figure 10.1.

Remember that this time supplements classroom assistance. Tier 2 interventions do not supplant the efforts of the classroom teacher, but enhance them.

Scheduling is the most obvious concern when pulling elementary school students out of their classrooms for Tier 2 interventions. Even the academic schedules of our youngest students are tightly packed from the moment they arrive until the very end of the day. Between increased state and federal mandates regarding the type of and time spent on the material taught, it seems that the amount of "down time" for students has diminished in recent years. This presents unique challenges when a student requires extra assistance in a critical subject area. The question becomes when to pull this student out to provide more intensive assistance. RTI allows a school to be certain that a student needs an intervention intensity increase. The RTI team would not recommend a student for Tier 2 services if the progress monitoring data did not warrant this. The problem becomes when to provide it.

There is no easy answer. The bottom line is that pulling any student out of class for anything—instrumental lessons, gifted-and-talented classes, supplemental instruction—creates a situation in which the student "misses" something that is occurring in the classroom. For a student who is attending a music lesson or a gifted-and-talented class, this trade-off is probably not an issue and, in the long run, the benefits most likely outweigh any potential consequences. For a student receiving supplemental instruction, this is not always the case. A student who is struggling to learn to read cannot afford to miss language arts instruction. Additionally, in many cases, this struggle in language arts can spill over into mathematics, so missing instruction in this area is not appropriate either. This dichotomy creates a situation in which building leaders need to be creative and look for solutions that have the least negative impacts. There is no perfect solution, so it becomes necessary to minimize the adverse impact as much as possible.

One place to identify possible pull-out time in the elementary day is during science and social studies instruction. This is not meant to imply in any way that these subject areas are less important than language arts and mathematics. However, there are a few important facts to consider. First, many times a student's struggles in language-arts literacy makes other reading-based subjects difficult as well. Reading and writing in the content areas are skills in and of themselves, and it is often easier to develop these skills in a small group rather than in a whole class setting. Students who have to miss science or social studies instruction to receive supplemental instruction should never miss out on the content of the material covered. That said, teachers and building-level leaders may want to make some decisions about excusing supplemental students from some of the less vital work that they miss. Many times, educators get hung up on every student completing every assignment regardless of the situation. In an RTI setting, it is imperative to remember that the goal is to improve academic ability and close the gap as soon as possible. Educators must make whatever accommodations are necessary to achieve this goal.

Another possibility for scheduling Tier 2 interventions can be found in the language arts literacy block itself. Many elementary literacy blocks set aside a significant amount of time in which students engage in independent activities. A prime example of this is when students are working in centers and the teacher is calling guided reading groups for small-group instruction. It is imperative that Tier 2 students do not miss their guided reading lesson, as this is presented on their instructional level. However, the center work in which they would participate is probably on grade level, which is currently beyond their reach. This center time is a great opportunity for an interventionist to pull this student from the classroom for instruction that is on the student's level and pushes him or her to reach a little higher. The important key to remember is this: All students need to have instruction from the teacher at their instructional level, and all students need to be exposed to grade-level appropriate text read aloud by a competent reader. Tier 2 students are certainly no exception. Those who decide schedules need to keep these key elements in mind and plan accordingly. There is no perfect solution, but if they work together, the professionals looking out for the Tier 2 students can make quality decisions that meet everyone's needs.

Challenges continue with the middle school schedule. Here, more dynamic and creative solutions for "finding time" are required. Can the students receive help during lunch time? Are there any "extra periods" that a staff member could be assigned to for intervention? Are there opportunities before school or after school? On certain days, can an in-class support teacher set aside 30 minutes to leave the primary assignment and work as an interventionist? Remember that interventions are only going to last as long as they are needed—such intervention plans may not require a full year. One criticism of such interventions is that a student misses too much classroom instruction during the intervention time. This is a fair criticism, however there are certain realities. One reality is that we have our students for a limited amount of time. Another reality is that fixing foundation literacy and numeracy skills is paramount for future student success. It is a matter of spending the limited time on the most important things; tough choices must be made. It is true that the student is going to miss something, but getting the student the necessary skills to succeed on their own must be the first priority.

What Tier 2 Interventions Should Be

Tier 2 interventions play a pivotal role in the RTI system. To reach this point, we have acknowledged that our efforts to date have failed to provide an adequate response from the student. We have acknowledged that we are willing to sacrifice our "least restrictive environment" to some degree to provide more intensive intervention. We are also handing over some direct responsibility for the child's growth to a professional other than the classroom teacher. This is significant as it means that the Reading Specialist or basic skills instructor who is now going to deliver Tier 2 interventions needs to bring something else to the table. Logistically, they are creating an environment that may facilitate greater learning opportunities through small group size, focused topics, and, potentially, a less distracting physical environment. If a school district has adequately invested in its professional development, these interventionists will bring specific knowledge and abilities to diagnose and remediate the issues. As we discussed in chapter 4, the importance of expert teachers to delivery intervention cannot be understated.

So, we have made the decision to move a child to Tier 2. What should a Tier 2 intervention look like? Consider the following characteristics.

Tier 2 interventions should be remedial in nature. Prior to an RTI system being in place, decisions about whether a student needed "extra help" would often be based on classroom assessments. In other words, it would be about grades. When a student earns poor grades, the student becomes frustrated, the teacher is concerned, and the parents get upset. The move to have a child seek "extra help" from an interventionist is meant to alleviate all of this anguish, so the primary goal of an interventionist becomes raising a student's grades. The best way to raise a student's grades is to prepare them for the assessment. Let's illustrate this through a vignette.

> Mr. O'Bryan gives a reading test at the end of every week. The reading test incorporates the vocabulary, spelling, and elements of that week's story selection. One of his students, Bradley, has been struggling on these assessments, particularly on the comprehension portion. Mr. O'Bryan is concerned, Bradley is frustrated, and Bradley's parents are upset. Mr. O'Bryan arranges for Bradley to get "extra help" from the school's Reading Specialist. The Reading Specialist wants Bradley to perform better on the end-of-selection assessment so, knowing what the story will be next week, they work on the story together. The Reading Specialist will read the story with Bradley, have Bradley read it back, pair Bradley with another student to partner read, and have Bradley listen to the story on tape. At the end of the week, Bradley passes his test! His teacher is less concerned, his parents are less upset, and Bradley is less frustrated.

This may or may not go on in your school, but believe us, we have seen this everywhere. The main problem is that nowhere in this scenario were Bradley's deficiencies diagnosed, nor were they addressed with remedial interventions. Bradley learned nothing that could be transferred to the next week's story, and he will continue to need "extra help." This is what creates the "gold-card holders." These are students who need help at an early age, and continue to need help throughout their academic careers because we never *teach* them, we only *tutor* them. A secondary problem is that we run a great risk of destroying any joy Bradley will associate with reading because we are drilling a story into him. What fun is that?

Tier 2 interventions need to be remedial, not simply extra help. They require an expert teacher who has the proper tools to diagnose the underlying causes of the difficulty, and who will address them directly. By teaching a student the skills they are missing, we provide them with transferrable skills to become better readers. You can translate this vignette to any subject matter. Drills and practice can make better test scores, but on their own they will never make a better student. This requires patience on the part of all of the stakeholders mentioned above. A student who is one to two years behind in his or her reading ability will not earn better grades immediately after seeing the Reading Specialist. It will take time, and the classroom teacher, the student, and the parents must all understand this. Their patience will pay off when the student can autonomously read and comprehend grade-level material.

Tier 2 interventions should be targeted in nature. Tier 2 interventions cannot be global to a grade level, or even to a marking period. There can be no standardized scope and sequence developed. Each student must be diagnosed independently and have their needs dictate the intervention and strategies used. This is another problem with any commercial product that suggests that it is a Response to Intervention program. These programs will want you to identify a level at which to start the child, and then proceed through a prescribed series of lessons. It is very possible that many of these programs offer good materials, but they cannot diagnose and prescribe like an expert teacher can. Once an expert teacher has determined a child's existing problems and the required interventions, any materials, "kits," or programs are simply tools from which the expert teacher can choose.

Tier 2 interventions should be fluid in nature. Tier 2 interventions cannot follow a prescribed path. The interventionist should expect to make changes in the materials used, the interventions tried, and the approaches taken as they learn more about a student. This has to be taken into consideration during an RTI team meeting. Eight weeks can sound like a very long time, but it is also a very short time to expect an interventionist to diagnose, intervene, monitor, and adjust. Struggling students will present an endless number of mysteries to solve and riddles to ponder. With each meeting, the interventionist learns more and more about the underlying causes of the difficulties and therefore can plot the course to address them. This fluidity will take time, but will often result in huge benefits.

The classroom teacher should support Tier 2 interventions. Tier 2 interventions supplement classroom instruction. Even though we have moved to Tier 2, we do not want to inadvertently take away any service that the classroom instruction provided because we have moved to Tier 2. If Bradley was receiving individualized centers and differentiated homework in Tier 1, it does not make sense for those interventions to stop when he moves to Tier 2. The combination of both sets of intervention can be very powerful. In fact, there may be adjustments made to the Tier 1 interventions based on the information that the specialist gathers in the Tier 2 environment. Good communication between the classroom teacher and the interventionist is essential to enhance both areas of instruction. The only transfer of responsibility in the move from Tier 1 to Tier 2 is the progress monitoring. The teacher providing the most intensive intervention tier should monitor the student's progress. Aside from that, everyone is still responsible for this child's success.

A Story of Struggling Kindergarteners

In our travels we have seen many similar patterns across districts , and they simply do not make sense. This is not a criticism of others; we realize that we are often looking into a mirror when we encounter such problems. This is a criticism of long-held, rarely evaluated practices. There are many of these in education. We often repeat behaviors because that is the way they have been done in the past; questioning them simply does not even cross our minds. How often do schools invite a speaker for an in-service day without offering follow-up training or changing expectations? How can a principal provide meaningful feedback when observing a teacher's execution of a new program if the principal only receives cursory training in the practice? Why do we suspend a child who repeats the same infraction despite being suspended before? You are probably coming up with several in your mind right now. How about this one: Why do we provide the least amount of intervention for the youngest students? This story reflects a situation that we have seen in many districts, including our own prior to RTI.

> Eric turned five in early September, entering half-day kindergarten just after his birthday party. He struggled with the demands of a school day and had difficulty with sharing the attention of the teacher, staying on task, and following class rules. Eric arrived at school as an average student (at best) and his immaturity quickly put him at academic risk. His teacher tried to give him extra attention, but so many children need so much attention in September of kindergarten. There was only so much of the teacher to go around! Seeing his academic challenges, Eric's teacher wanted to get him some extra help. However, interventions for kindergarteners were virtually non-existent. The Reading Specialist's time was devoted to older students, after-school programs were reserved for full-day students, and the only additional "pair of hands" to help in kindergarten was a paraprofessional. Eric would struggle through kindergarten, try to play "catch-up" in first grade, and finally get to see the specialist in second or third grade, long after his academic challenges had cemented into genuine difficulties.

If this sounds familiar to you, trust us, you are not alone. We have encountered school districts that do not allow kindergarteners to be brought before a Student Intervention Team, do not have supplemental programs for them outside of the classroom or school day, do not have summer programs for them, and do not have certified staff that provide intervention until later grades. Some districts will not even consider special education classification for kindergarteners. In a recent article for *Education Week's Teacher PD*

Sourcebook, early literacy expert Richard Allington spoke to this saying, "But you have to look around and ask, how many schools do we currently have that have any kind of intensive expert intervention in place in kindergarten, much less 30 or 45 minutes a day of one-to-one or one-to-three expert intervention for up to a year in the 1st grade? The answer is, there are virtually no schools like that in this country." Thirty to 45 minutes a day, one-to-one, or one-to-three expert interventions qualify as Tier 3 interventions. From what we have seen in our travels, Dr. Allington is correct—this type of intervention does not exist. But this is exactly the time it should exist. Imagine the resources that would become available and the time that could be saved and devoted to other causes if early interventions were successful and future help was not necessary. There is also a significant benefit for the students themselves if we intervene aggressively during the critical years of language acquisition.

System Responsibilities of the Interventionist

Obviously, the primary responsibility of the Interventionist is to diagnose and remediate the challenges that the student is facing. From a RTI structure standpoint, the interventionist is also responsible for several items.

In many school settings that we have encountered, a basic skills teacher or a Reading Specialist who is adding a student to his or her caseload is responsible for contacting the parents. This can be the same in an RTI setting as well. However, such communication should not be a surprise to the parent. Parents should be aware that their child was in something called "Tier 1" They should understand what "adequate response to intervention" means, and they should know what will happen if the school determines that their child needs more intensive assistance. Regardless, anytime that a student is removed from the classroom setting for instruction, it is essential that parents are notified and introduced to the interventionist. The RTI team may facilitate this process, if so desired.

The interventionist is also responsible for progress monitoring once the student is in Tier 2. The interventionist will give weekly probes and record the scores in the monitoring software. This will provide the interventionist with immediate feedback as he or she interacts with the child in an assessment environment each week. It allows the interventionist to see any developing trends before the progress monitoring cycle ends, and it also lets them make necessary adjustments before the RTI team meeting dates.

The interventionist is also responsible for documenting all pertinent information about the interventions used, including the frequency, duration, and type. This is similar to the documentation required of the classroom teacher in Tier 1. The information is submitted to the RTI team for consideration and discussion. It also provides a journal of strategies and comments on which the interventionist can reflect.

Can In-class Support be a Tier 2 Intervention?

This question comes up when we are asked if an in-class support setting should be considered a Tier 1 or a Tier 2 intervention. The answer is that it has little to do with the physical setting because a change in tier only concerns the intensity of the intervention. An in-class support setting can be a Tier 1 or a Tier 2 intervention, or it can be neither. The simple presence of an additional teacher does not make a classroom "default" to a tier. Consider some examples:

An in-class support classroom (ICS) has two teachers assigned to it since there are three students with ICS individualized education programs (IEPs) in the class every day. After the second Universal Screening a previously non-tier student is identified as needing intervention. Someone may make a comment such as, "The student has been in an in-class support setting all year. Shouldn't that 'count' as Tier 1? Therefore, shouldn't we move him right to Tier 2?" The answer is, "Absolutely not!" The mere presence of an additional teacher does not mean that this student has received targeted, deliberate assistance, nor has any progress been monitored.

In the above example, could the in-class support teacher now provide Tier 1 interventions to the newly identified student? The answer is yes, provided that there are deliberate and targeted interventions put in place for the student.

Continuing the storyline, suppose the student does not respond adequately to the Tier 1 interventions. Could the student move to Tier 2 and still receive those interventions in the classroom? Again, the answer is yes, with some important qualifiers. First, it is assumed that Tier 1 interventions were adequately assessed and modified when the student failed to respond. Second, it is imperative that the intervention's intensity increase significantly if we are to call it a Tier 2 intervention. We cannot allow the same interventions to simply be labeled differently. For example, suppose that within the in-class support classroom, the Tier 1 interventions were individualized centers and differentiated homework. Suppose these interventions did not provide the adequate response we were looking for, so we doubled the guided reading time for the Tier 1 student's reading group. Failing to find adequate response at this point may indicate a need to change tiers. The RTI team could keep the student in the classroom with the Tier 1 interventions while also providing additional intervention. This would constitute a move to Tier 2. Perhaps the individualized centers could be replaced with additional small group instruction with one of the teachers during center time. Perhaps another time during the day could provide an opportunity for additional support.

One important caveat on this scenario: Should these in-class Tier 2 interventions not encourage adequate growth for the student, this student should not be moved to Tier 3 until interventions outside the classroom have been tried.

11

What Happens if Tier 2 Doesn't Work?

The system is in place. A Universal Screening tool has quickly identified a student that has potential for academic difficulty, and research-based interventions were swiftly implemented. The educators involved tried to address the student's challenges through Tier 1 interventions in the classroom, which is the least restrictive environment possible. However, the student's response was not adequate, so the child began to receive supplementary assistance outside the classroom (a Tier 2 intervention). But the student is still not closing the identified skill and ability gaps. What now? Students who do not show adequate response to Tier 2 interventions will be moved to Tier 3.

How Does a Student Get Into Tier 3?

There is only one way for a student to get into Tier 3. This occurs when the RTI team determines that interventions have been implemented faithfully for a reasonable (and standardized) amount of time, but the student is still not responding adequately. This is a critical decision for several reasons. First, the student has received Tier 2 interventions for at least one progress monitoring cycle (eight weeks in our structure), and possibly more. Moving the student to Tier 2 was already a very big decision since it was the first time that the RTI team determined that the child should see an outside-class specialist in a more restrictive environment. The potential complications of such a move are familiar to us all: the possible feeling of failure on the part of the student, the concerns of the parents, the in-class instruction the student will miss during their pull-out time, the additional complication when scheduling the groups, and so forth. When this substantial effort still does not show results, it is a lot for everyone to process. Second, Tier 3 interventions require a huge invest-ment of resources, especially in terms of the time spent by the specialist who will work with the student. As we will shortly define, Tier 3 requires that a specialist meet with fewer students (this means one-on-one meetings in some cases), and for a greater amount of time. This is a very significant investment of resources. Third, the RTI team will be very cognizant of the fact that there are no more tiers after Tier 3. The looming prospect of a special education referral is on the horizon, and the RTI team will begin to feel the pressure of answering the question, "Have we done all we can do?" prior to such a step.

Because of the aforementioned reasons, the RTI team should look criti-cally at altering the Tier 2 interventions within the Tier 2 structure before declaring that tier inadequate. The team needs to determine if the time con-straints of Tier 2 are part of the issue, or if other interventions can be tried within the Tier 2 structure. There will be times when the answer to those questions point to a need for more intensive intervention, which usually requires more time spent, a smaller group size, and more frequent meetings. The "move-in" exception (the exception made for students who are new to the school or district) to assigning a student to Tier 2 exists for Tier 3 as well, but it should be used with extreme caution since this means that the school may only attempt intervention once before considering a special education referral. That potentially poses a great deal of difficulty for a student who has just moved into the district.

Once again, scheduling becomes a major concern when dealing with Tier 3 students. The issue becomes even more difficult because the time the inter-vention sessions require increases dramatically between Tier 2 and Tier 3. Scheduling such interventions can seem daunting at best, but it is important to remember a few key facts about Tier 3 before becoming too frustrated. First, the number of Tier 3 students is very likely to be low. Most students can be adequately assisted in Tier 1 or Tier 2 , so only the neediest students move onto the third level. Scheduling at Tier 3 happens on an individual basis, which gives school leaders plenty of flexibility. Second, when a stu-dent does reach Tier 3 for a reading issue, there is nothing more important than providing the student with all possible resources to learn to read more successfully. A Tier 3 student has significant difficulties that neither the class-room teacher's extra efforts nor an outside-class professional's thrice weekly interventions could improve. Whatever issues the student is facing are sig-nificantly impacting his or her educational experience, and most likely affect all areas of the child's academic day. School leaders need to manipulate the schedule however they are able in order to provide adequate services. Finally, it is important to remember that the step following Tier 3 is a referral to spe-cial education services. The decision to move down this road should never be taken lightly, and creative scheduling ideas should always be put into play before choosing this path. While educators should follow the same guidelines used for scheduling Tier 2 interventions whenever possible, Tier 3 students are unique in the fact that the services they require are paramount to their academic survival.

What are Tier 3 Interventions?

The purpose of Tier 3 interventions is to intensify the Tier 2 intervention by providing a specialized environment for the student and his or her certified interventionist. It should allow for three factors: more time, more attention, and greater frequency. The intervention itself may or may not change. This is a decision for the interventionist considering the individual student. There are certainly materials and programs designed for one-to-one instruction, but these are just more "tools in the toolkit" for the interventionist to choose from. It is certainly possible for the interventionist to believe that he or she simply needs more time in a smaller setting with the student.

As with Tier 2, the teachers who are the primary providers of Tier 3 interventions will be the staff members who do not have primary classroom responsibilities. Instead, the Tier 3 interventionists are those who are typically charged with assisting struggling children, such as Reading Specialists, special education teachers, and basic skills instructors. Tier 3 interventions will continue to remove a student from his or her classroom to meet with a small group of students, or possibly one-to-one with their interventionist. Compare the guidelines for the frequency, duration, and group size between Tier 2 and Tier 3 as summarized in Figure 11.1.

Remember that this time still supplements assistance in the classroom. Tier 3 interventions do not supplant the classroom teacher's efforts, and it is critical that the teacher continue his or her efforts in the regular setting.

What Tier 3 Interventions Should Be

If you have reached this point in the book by reading all the way through, you know that we are not going to endorse a single program or a practice that should be the only tool used in any and all tiers. Instead, we must continue to emphasize the critical nature of professional development within an RTI system. As students move through the tiers, they must receive more time, more attention, and greater frequency. They also need to receive that time and attention from expertly trained teachers. It is possible to have one teacher provide Tier 2 and Tier 3 interventions for the same student, but it is also very

FIGURE 11.1 Tier 2-Tier 3 Comparison

Intervention	Frequency	Duration	Number of Students
Tier 2	3 times a week or "every other day"	Minimum of 30 minutes	4 to 6 students
Tier 3	Up to 5 times a week	Minimum of 45 minutes, up to 60 minutes	1 to 3 students

possible to have the Tier 2 teacher "hand off" responsibility for the student as the child moves to Tier 3. This is a decision that may be based on schedules and availability, but it also may be a decision based on the particular training or expertise of the teachers. If you are going to try a specific intervention with students in Tier 3, it would be best to place them with your most experienced and talented teacher in that intervention. This also suggests that the administration should provide a variety of training for their interventionists. This increases the number of "tools in the toolbox" for the school as a whole. If a school has one specialist who is specially trained in a phonics-based intervention and has another trained in a skill- based intervention, a school will have great latitude when matching student needs to available tools.

It is essential that the four characteristics of Tier 2 interventions remain constant when applied to Tier 3 interventions. There is a more detailed description of these characteristics in the previous chapter, but they are:

Tier 3 interventions should be remedial in nature. Tier 3 interventions need to be remedial, not the "extra help" we warned against in chapter 10. Interventions designed to remediate require an expert teacher with the proper tools for diagnosing and directly addressing the underlying causes of the difficulty. By Tier 3, we are trying to get a student "back from the brink" by remediating the crucial skills that the students need to build upon.

Tier 3 interventions should be targeted in nature. Just as interventions increase in strength as a student moves from Tier 2 to Tier 3, so, too, do the intensity of the associated descriptors and warnings. Tier 3 interventions MUST be targeted in nature because we are working with such a small percentage of our students, investing so heavily in their growth, and have learned so much about their challenges, gaps, and difficulties over the course of Tier 1 and Tier 2 intervention time. Each student MUST be diagnosed independently and have his or her needs dictate the intervention and strategies used.

Tier 3 interventions should be fluid in nature. As with Tier 2 interventions, Tier 3 interventions cannot follow a prescribed path. The interventionist should expect to make changes in the materials used, the interventions tried, and the approaches taken as they continue to learn more about the student.

Tier 3 interventions should be supported by the classroom teacher. As always, any intervention that takes place outside of the classroom must be done with the knowledge and support of the classroom teacher. There will be countless opportunities throughout the school day for the teacher to highlight and reinforce the skills and abilities that the interventionist is addressing. These are the authentic opportunities that provide additional practice for the student and additional feedback for the teachers. It can also provide an opportunity for genuine growth in confidence as the student performs some task in front of his or her regular classroom peers.

Multi-Disciplinary Team Involvement

The Individuals with Disabilities Education Act (IDEA) refers to a "group of qualified professionals" who determine eligibility for special education services. Regardless of what your state calls this team (in New Jersey it is called the Child Study Team), these individuals are responsible for any testing and decision-making that is done as part of special education eligibility determinations. One of the core beliefs of RTI that we noted in chapter 4 was creating a seamless transition from regular education interventions to special education interventions. As we place students in Tier 3 interventions, we approach that stage where the absence of "seamless integration" would be most keenly felt. Without an RTI system that acknowledges the relationship between Tier 3 interventions and special education services, it could appear to parents and students (as well as teachers and administrators) that a passing of responsibility takes place when a student is classified as eligible for special education. This is a horrible mistake and does a great disservice to the student. We want our special education services to work in conjunction with our regular education services. We want our students to remain in the least restrictive environment as much as possible, and feel success in their regular classroom. We want skills learned and honed in the special education settings to transfer over to the regular classroom. All of this requires the mindset that everyone is responsible for every child; that there is never a "hand off" of responsibility for a child's success.

To help facilitate this "seamless integration," the RTI system needs to bring the Child Study Team (CST) into the mix as students enter Tier 3. To do this, the RTI structure requires that one member of the CST act as a liaison to the RTI team. Once a student is in Tier 3, this liaison will receive the weekly progress monitoring data from the interventionist involved with the student. This is different from Tier 1 or Tier 2 practices in which progress monitoring reports are provided only to the RTI team at the end of the eight week progress monitoring cycle. By providing weekly reports to the CST liaison, interactions between the special education staff and the teachers can begin to take place. The Child Study Team member can make suggestions to the interventionist, questions can be asked of the classroom teacher, and the interventionist can solicit ideas. This communication can be very powerful on several fronts. First, no student will ever receive a special education referral without everyone being aware of the concerns for at least eight weeks. The student's strengths and weaknesses, the previous attempts to remediate, the classroom teacher's concerns, and any extenuating factors will all be known. Second, the teacher and the interventionist will not feel second-guessed when a third party comes in (after weeks or months of attempted interventions) to say that not enough was done prior to referral. The RTI structure will regularly facilitate communication, so everyone will know what is happening. Third, since the CST members were part of the efforts all along, they will know that every attempt prior to a special education referral has been faithfully tried. This is particularly important when discussing special education options with parents. Fourth, this interaction supports the powerful message to all staff members that regular education staff, intervention staff, and special education staff are truly all part of the same team and are all collectively responsible for every child.

What Happens if a Child in Tier 3 Shows an Inadequate Response to Intervention?

If Tier 3 does not result in adequate response to intervention, the RTI team has two choices. First, they can repeat another cycle of Tier 3 interventions, perhaps to give it more time or to "tweak" the intervention. This would be the opportunity to move from 45 minutes to 60 minutes of intervention, or from a one-to-three environment to a one-to-one environment. This would also be the opportunity to change the intervention within the same time and frequency of meetings. Or, it could be time to refer the child to the multi-disciplinary team and begin the process of determining eligibility for special services.

A Word on Retention

Retaining a student in the same grade for another year is a topic that gen-erates very diverse opinions and can lead to heated debates. We do not wish to enter that debate in this book. Instead, we would like to frame retention in a way that we all (or maybe just most of us) can agree on. We would like to assume the following regarding a decision to retain a child:

1. That the ultimate goal of the retention is to increase the chances that the student will be successful in the long term.
2. That the decision to retain assumes that the student will be better prepared for the next grade after repeating this grade than he or she would be if promoted.
3. That other interventions provided in a promotion year will not be as successful as the retention.

Assuming that the above is considered fair, we would like to suggest that a decision to retain is, in itself, an *intervention* on behalf of the student in the same way that providing supplemental assistance through the tier system is an intervention. Considering the potential for emotional stress and self-esteem damage that retention may inflict, we assume that we can agree that retention would be considered a significant, if not drastic, level of intervention.

With all of this in mind, we suggest that retention decisions based on academic concerns should lie solely with the RTI team, and could only be utilized in a situation where the student did not have an adequate response to Tier 3 interventions. If a student did not have tier interventions, then the child should not be considered for such a significant one before less intrusive ones have been attempted. If the student is currently in a tier and receiving inter-ventions, he or she should be afforded every opportunity to show progress prior to such a decision. If the child is currently in Tier 3 and is responding to the interventions, the student should be promoted with a continuation of Tier 3 interventions in their new grade.

What if They Don't Qualify for Special Education Services?

So, you have done everything right. The student was identified early, you intervened aggressively, they moved through the tiers appropriately, but a special education eligibility referral was the course that had to be taken. In many districts, testing would take place and the discrepancy formula for eligibility would determine the next steps. What if this child does not qualify under these rules? That can be a significant problem because the school has basically told the special education team, "We gave it everything we have." What now? There are two answers to this question, and both are considerably assisted by the integration of the special and regular education staff mentioned above. First, there are other methods of determining eligibility for special education services besides the discrepancy formula. Your Child Study Team (or equivalent team) will know how to classify a student as special education under the RTI rules of IDEA, or via a functional assessment of the child's abilities. Second, the decision may be to not classify based on the testing. In this case, it would be the CST's responsibility to meet with the RTI team, the interventionists, and the classroom teacher to discuss a new Tier 3 intervention plan that could be more effective for the student. This again goes back to the idea that every staff member is responsible for every child. If special education services are not available for whatever reason (remember, parents can refuse to sign IEPs), then the school must still do all it can for any student.

12

How Do I Get Started in My District?

As we have noted time and time again, change is a very difficult undertaking. It is especially challenging when the ideals that need to be altered revolve around long-standing beliefs and procedures. For many schools, this is the exact scenario they will face when trying to move to a Response to Intervention method of providing supplemental services to struggling students. When this occurs, often the hardest part is knowing where to start. While every district has unique qualities and situations, most schools share very common features, and one group's journey can provide a very solid road map to get another started down its own path.

Our journey began by assembling a small group of interested stakeholders from various positions within the district. This committee was chaired by the Assistant Superintendent for Curriculum and Instruction and was comprised of building-level principals, the Supervisor of Resource Center and Pre-Referral Services, a psychologist, a learning disability specialist, two Reading Specialists, a special education teacher, and a regular education teacher. The wide variety of perspectives was very valuable because each person's knowledge and experience caused them to create different questions and raise different concerns as discussions began. For example, the regular education classroom teacher had strong opinions on what was and was not feasible for those individuals who had the sole responsibility for 25 primary grade students each day. The Reading Specialists were able to share their expansive knowledge regarding what types of interventions were most successful in which situations. Building administrators were able to provide guidance about what structure was needed, and how best to implement the philosophies and ideas developed by the group as a whole. Losing the knowledge of any one of these groups would have significantly slowed down the progress of the initiative as a whole.

It is important to note one other issue related to the formation of this initial committee. The members of this group predominantly represented the general education realm. This was not our intention when we began our journey, but in retrospect it was something that, in the end, was a large contributor to our success. Staff members who work predominantly in the general education realm often have a discomfort related to special education practices and procedures. This discomfort tends to come from a lack of understanding and often results in regular education teachers relinquishing responsibility for a student once the child is classified as special education. If an RTI model is simply seen as the first step in the classification process, many staff members involved in regular education may not feel a strong sense of responsibility toward the identified students. Since a primary goal of an RTI model is to remediate academic issues prior to the need for special education services, it is imperative that all staff members take an active role in providing substantial interventions and invest themselves in their results. While the special educator's expertise is invaluable in an RTI model, the initiative must be identified as regular education in order to be most successful.

The importance of this initial committee becomes apparent immediately because there are many big decisions to make that will influence the entire RTI initiative, as well as its chances for success. The first four decisions can be listed very concisely, but they have overwhelming importance and influence. The committee must be in agreement on:

◆ The core beliefs of the Response to Intervention model that will ultimately guide all other decisions
◆ A tier structure for interventions
◆ The Universal Screening and progress monitoring tools that will be used
◆ The grade levels that will be used for the initial implementation

Establishing the core beliefs of the district's Response to Intervention model requires an extensive amount of research and discussion. The principles established here will guide all other decisions and will serve as the hallmarks of the entire initiative. These ideals will promote consistency among schools and allow a faithful implementation to occur. When will your district start screening to determine if there are potential concerns? What will occur once a potential concern is identified? How often will you monitor your students' progress? How will the new RTI structure integrate with the classification procedures already in place? These questions will determine your district's core beliefs and allow procedural decisions to fall into place.

The tier structure for interventions is the next piece of the puzzle that must be defined. While the philosophical decisions made when determining the core beliefs are critical to the initiative's ultimate success, there is no substitution for strong procedural support. How many tiers must a student pass through before being referred to the Child Study Team for classification? How will you determine if a student is responding adequately to an intervention, or if that intervention needs to be intensified? How much time will a student spend in each tier before decisions need to be made? Our district found it best to illustrate the tier structure agreed upon in flowchart form. This format allowed all users to easily understand how tiers were connected and who was responsible for what at each point during the process. It is imperative to note how important it is for the new RTI structure's philosophy to be clearly illustrated in a usable format so implementation can occur easily.

Following the tier structure decisions comes the choice of a screening tool. What will your district use as a tool for Universal Screening and progress monitoring? There are many products that can serve this purpose. It is important to consider the research behind the selected tool, as well as the ease of use for teachers and the amount of time that it will take away from instruction. The screening tool chosen is one of the first attributes of RTI visible to the staff who will implement the model. It is imperative to keep this in mind when making this selection.

An implementation schedule is the final key decision that the initial committee needs to make. It is impossible to implement a program of this magnitude in all applicable grade levels at one time. If a district wants to significantly change the way the staff views supplemental instruction for struggling students, the move to RTI needs to come with adequate training and time to implement it. Our initial decision to implement the model in kindergarten through second grade allowed us to focus our limited resources and make the most of them, while still having an impact on the students who needed assistance the most.

Once the district has established a core set of beliefs and a configuration to accommodate the tier structure, it is time to begin the process of philosophy "buy-in." The core group of professionals who have worked on the initiative since its inception certainly believe in its necessity. Now it is time to include the next circle of stakeholders. In every district there are certain key players who have the ability to make an initiative a success or a failure simply by expressing their opinion. These people must be identified and introduced to the progress the district has made thus far while working toward an RTI model. Other building administrators, Reading Specialists, union leaders, lead teachers, and so forth all need to be informed about RTI and the advantages this system would bring to the children the district serves. Without their support, an initiative will not go anywhere.

Consistency is the most important aspect of this "buy-in" process. In larger districts, it is often very difficult to ensure that all schools are implementing a new program in the intended manner. The implementation of RTI is no different. Since RTI is a change in philosophy as well as procedure, the people presenting the new information to the staff need to be sure they have interpreted the concepts and ideals in the same manner. For example, once the transition to an RTI model was complete in our district, the only way a student could receive supplemental services was by starting in Tier 1 as the result of the Universal Screening, or through the Request for Review of Records form. This is a key component of both our RTI philosophy and structure. If this is not communicated clearly to all stakeholders, the integrity of the whole program comes into question.

Once the circle of interested stakeholders has been expanded, it is time to involve more people in the decision-making process. The basic structure flowchart now needs to be infused with many details. Which staff members will monitor students' progress at each tier? How will you train the staff members responsible for administering progress monitoring probes? What additional documentation (besides the scores generated by the assessment) will you require of the staff administering the progress monitoring? Who delivers the instruction at each tier in the model? What changes will need to be made to the master schedule to accommodate the changes in use of interventionists? What materials and training will the instructors at each tier need? How will Tier 2 and Tier 3 interventions be delivered in middle school? While this list of questions may seem daunting at first, the answers are generally straightforward once the initial procedural flowchart has been developed. It is imperative that the answers to all of these questions support the underlying philosophies that are guiding the district's RTI initiative.

Along with the decisions regarding the tier structure and progress monitoring are decisions associated with Universal Screening. A district needs to decide which staff members will be responsible for administering the Universal Screening. Educators should also decide how to best facilitate the screening's administration within each individual school's parameters. Keep in mind that all students in the impacted grade levels go through the Universal Screening process, so it is a big undertaking that requires proper planning. As with progress monitoring, decisions must be made regarding how and when various staff members will be trained to administer these assessments.

As you plan for the training of the staff who will administer the Universal Screenings and progress monitoring probes, it is vital to trust in the quality of the screening tool that the district selected. If the initial decision-making committee has spent adequate time and done enough research, you can trust that it will serve the students of your district well.

As we researched appropriate assessments for our Response to Intervention model, we were very concerned with four issues: time, cost, ease of use, and whether or not the assessment was researched-based in nature. After looking into many products, we settled on DIBELS out of the University of Oregon. The DIBELS assessments were one minute in length so it would not take long to screen every child. The cost was $1 per student—a very reasonable fee in this educational climate. The directions for each assessment were easy to understand, and the district felt confident that we could teach our staff how to administer the tests with fidelity. The University of Oregon had been using DIBELS as part of its research into early literacy, and it had used the data collected from hundreds of thousands of students over time. It met all of our criteria, and we felt very confident that we were headed in the right direction.

Members of the initial committee were trained in administering DIBELS assessments. They would then teach the information to a small group of Reading Specialists, and other interventionists in the district. This select group of eight people would then turnkey it to others in their building, and eventually all the necessary staff would be able to accurately assess their students using the DIBELS measures.

On the first day of training for the group of eight, we started with the kindergarten test entitled, "Letter Naming Fluency." The test is comprised of a single sheet of randomized letters. The student being assessed is to move from letter to letter naming each as they go. Their score is simply the number of letters named correctly in the span of one minute. The training was going as well as could be expected, and since this test was simple, everyone was catching on very quickly.

About three minutes into our "practice" time, a teacher called me over and expressed concern over the way the very first letter was printed on the page. The lower case letter "a" was written in a typed style ("a") as opposed to the traditional "ɑ" used in kindergarten. This innocent comment led to a fifteen-minute discussion during which many of the instructors in the session (including myself) seriously considered creating our own sheet and changing the materials provided by the University of Oregon.

Finally, the voice of reason stepped in and reminded us that one of the reasons we selected the University of Oregon's materials in the first place was the strong research-base that supported them. We needed to trust in the decision we had made and know that the materials would supply us with the information we needed to make quality decisions about our students. The letters were left as they were intended on the DIBELS materials, and we have been using them in our district ever since.

It is important to remember that we must give the materials we select for initiatives, such as RTI, an opportunity to work. This means using them in the manner in which they were intended to be used. So often in education, we are looking for that "quick fix," and when results are not immediate or when something does not jive with what we feel is appropriate, we simply dismiss it because we believe that we know better. Our district took the time to do our homework and select a research-based product that met our needs. Our decision to trust in this product has proven to be invaluable as we have moved forward on our journey.

There is one other essential decision that needs to be made when planning the Universal Screening portion of your RTI model. The Response to Intervention structure is set up in such a way that the only path to supplemental services is through Tier 1 interventions in the regular education classroom. The most common way to recognize a Tier 1 student is through the scores received on the Universal Screening. Once a tool has been selected for use in this capacity, the district must determine what scores will result in a Tier 1 identification. In our case, we were able to use the recommendations made by the DIBELS software once we entered our data, but that may not be the case for every district. As a district begins a new RTI model, the governing body needs to decide where the line is for admittance to Tier 1. The placement of the line must consider the amount of staff available to provide intervention services, and the number of students who could possibly benefit from such assistance. Once the parameters are set, it is important to make sure they are adhered to, once again supporting the underlying RTI philosophy.

The next set of decisions that a school undertaking a new RTI model will face revolve around developing an implementation timeline. As noted before, educators will probably expect to see immediate results when they begin a new program. They are equally likely to expect that a new structure can be implemented flawlessly in a very short period of time. We have found that a large key to the success of our RTI model was due to the time we spent on implementation. While it is obvious that it takes a great deal of time to develop a functional RTI philosophy and set of procedures, there are many other areas in which patience is a requirement.

The first area that requires a great deal of time is the training of staff for the administration of the Universal Screening and progress monitoring tools. Teachers need to develop a comfort level with the supplies selected, and the only way to become proficient with the testing materials is to administer the test many times. While using an entire school year to train teachers and practice administering the prompts might seem tedious, the results are well worth the investment of time and energy. If staff members are given enough time to practice, the data collected during the first year of the RTI program will be reliable, and the people analyzing it will be able to use it to make quality decisions for the students they are serving.

The staff members who will provide interventions to the struggling students need professional development, and this will require a great deal of time. Thinking back to the core philosophies of our RTI model, there are no specific programs or practices prescribed for each tier or intervention. Instead, the teachers working with the struggling students need to determine what works best for each particular child's needs. If these staff members do not have a wide variety of tools at their disposal, the system falls apart and, ultimately, the child is the one who suffers. Teachers need to have access to quality, sustained professional development in the areas for which they will be providing intervention.

The strong desire to simply select an "RTI program" or pre-packaged set of materials is a pitfall that you must avoid. A large number of products on the market place "RTI" in their titles, and it is very tempting to select some of these items and assign them for use in a particular tier. While this strategy may add structure to an RTI model, it does not let the teacher have maximum influence. In order for the greatest success to occur, the teacher should be able to make decisions about what materials to use with which students in each individual circumstance. On the surface, this appears to many as if the creators of the RTI system are trying to skip the material selection step. However, in the long run the individual students, and the program as a whole, reap the benefits.

Decisions Specific to Middle School Implementation

Many of the decisions mentioned above apply to both elementary and middle school implementation. However, there are some additional questions that must be considered as your district constructs a middle school model. First, how will Tier 1 students be identified? As mentioned before, there will be a great deal of information available about a student in sixth grade. A grid or rubric that records points to determine the degree to which a student is "at risk" is a reasonable alternative to additional screening. Once a school identifies such students, it will need to conduct diagnostic assessments. However, that relieves a school from the "universal" part of screening, and it will save tremendous time and resources. Second, a school will need reliable and efficient diagnostic tools. Again, there are many commercial products available, or the district can create its own tools. Third, the "schedule masters" who manage calendars (every middle school has them!) need to help create time for Tier 2 and Tier 3 interventions to occur. Bring people together for a brainstorming session and you may be surprised the variety of options you brainstorm. For instance, some common suggestions may include spending time before or after school or during lunch; making inter-vention a "special;" or scheduling time on Saturdays. We are sure that your staff will be even more creative.

Of course, even after the most thorough planning and research, there will still be those who do not believe that a Response to Intervention model can adequately serve the struggling learners in your district. There is no way to anticipate every naysayer's question or comment, but there are quite a num-ber of themes that come up again and again. They have become myths about why an RTI structure will not be successful.

Myth Number 1: Our district does not have adequate staffing to sustain an RTI model. Every school district around the country already has numerous systems in place that provide extra services to struggling students who do not have a special education classification. In many schools, these people have specific titles such as Reading Specialist, basic skills instructor, in-class support teacher, or corrective reading teacher. In other settings, they may simply be called interventionists. Whatever the case may be, schools have staff members who provide these services to students. When a school imple-ments an RTI model, they just reallocate these teachers to either serve differ-ent students, or serve in different settings. Educational leaders implementing this type of model need to evaluate existing structures and see where it makes sense to shift staff. One word of caution when beginning this examination: It is most advantageous to have certified staff members working with the neediest students. Many times, less talented staff members are moved into settings where they see the fewest students and, in many cases, this means they move to supplemental education programs. If the tier structure is to suc-ceed, the students in the RTI system must have access to the highest quality instruction possible from the best teachers.

Myth Number 2: We will need to purchase massive amounts of materials to implement RTI successfully. There are materials that are necessary for a successful Response to Intervention program. As previously mentioned, a district needs to select an assessment tool for Universal Screening and prog-ress monitoring. A district also should be sure that all of the teachers working with struggling students have a wide variety of instructional tools available to best meet the needs of their students. That said, there are research-based Universal Screening tools available online, and there are other options that you can purchase at a relatively low cost. In terms of teacher training, many instructional tools that teachers need are more concerned with the quality of professional development offered instead of the quantity of materials pur-chased. While quality professional development can cost money, if a few key staff members attend trainings and then teach what they learn to others in the district, the money spent can have a large impact. Certainly some materials will always be necessary, but it is vital to remember that no single program or product will meet the needs of every child in the RTI system. Conversely, great teaching will.

Myth Number 3: There is not enough time in our current schedule to allow for a Response to Intervention model. The reality is that there is not enough time to fit in all the lessons we would like our children to have each day. Between daily routines, state-mandated programs, and various daily interruptions, it seems that the instructional day gets shorter and shorter all the time. In order to have a successful RTI model in your district, educational leaders need to try to reallocate the time available and make sure it is being used to its fullest advantage. For example, a second-grade student in Tier 2 or 3 who reads on a primer or pre-primer level will often be lost during a group lesson revolving around a read-aloud book. A person organizing the RTI schedule may want to pull this student out of this lesson and work with the child on his or her level. The student spends the same amount of time on reading instruction as the other students, but the instruction's emphasis has been altered to increase its effectiveness. Many times, students within the RTI tier system will have more reading instruction, especially when they reach Tier 3, but if more time is not available, the focus should be on making the time available more effective.

Myth Number 4: Our district does not need a Response to Intervention model because we already provide basic skills instruction to our neediest students. As mentioned earlier, most schools already have systems in place to assist their struggling students. What makes RTI different from the great majority of these programs is the progress monitoring component: Does the student's weekly progress monitoring data show that the interventions are actually improving his or her reading ability, or should something else be tried instead? In our district, once we identified students as needing extra help, they saw an interventionist a few times a week and primarily worked on the skills and concepts being covered in their classrooms. While this practice generally led to an improvement in classroom grades, it rarely led to increased reading ability. In order to "close the gap" and truly improve reading skills, students need to be exposed to materials and instructional strategies that cater to the areas in which they are weak; the progress monitoring data needs to be analyzed to see if there is improvement. The salient fact to remember here is that even when the progress monitoring data conclusively shows that the interventions are working, classroom grades might not necessarily reflect this. The ultimate goal is to close the skill gap, and it may take a good deal of time in order for the improvements shown in progress monitoring data to show up in classroom grades. Unless your current system contains a progress monitoring component, an RTI system will be superior.

Myth Number 5: **The parents in our district do not like change, and they will resist a move to a Response to Intervention model.** It is true that change in a school district can be very challenging for everyone involved. Administrators, teachers, students, and parents are all creatures of habit, and the path of least resistance is often the same as the road we have always traveled. The crucial element to a successful RTI implementation is twofold. First, always be transparent. When people ask about the new philosophy or structure, whether they are teachers or parents, answer their questions completely and honestly. When the ultimate goal is the betterment of our students, everyone has a difficult time objecting. Second, use the data collected as your evidence. There is nothing more powerful than showing a parent the progress monitoring graph of a student who is in a tier and improving significantly. The parent will be able to visually recognize the upward trend of the graph and will want the intervention to continue. Conversely, if a progress monitoring graph shows that an intervention is not having the desired impact, teachers and parents alike will want to seek a different approach. There is no reason to continue ineffective interventions.

Myth Number 6: **A Response to Intervention model is simply a means to increase the time it takes to get to a Child Study Team referral for special education classification.** Once again, it is important to go back and look at the cornerstones of our RTI beliefs. The model suggests that pre-referral interventions can work and special-education classification is not predetermined. The RTI model simply ensures that all viable regular education interventions have been tried and progress monitored prior to Child Study Team (CST) testing. Each progress monitoring cycle is only eight weeks in length, so it is possible for a child to enter Tier 1 and move through Tiers 2 and 3 within a 24-week period. While most children spend more than one cycle in Tier 2 or Tier 3, the time period is not unlimited. The goal is to make sure the correct students wind up with a CST evaluation, not to increase the time that passes to get to one.

There are two additional issues that have become paramount to our success with RTI, but we didn't necessarily realize their importance early on. The first is time. When the RTI model was unveiled to our eight elementary schools, one of the first pieces of information everyone wanted was a schedule of events. When would Universal Screenings take place? When would each progress monitoring block begin and end? When would RTI team meetings be held? All of these questions were answered by a district-created master calendar of events (see Chapter 8). Our school year is state-mandated to have at least 180 student days. This number lent itself very well to eight-week progress monitoring cycles, with Universal Screenings and RTI meetings built around them. Other models prescribe slightly longer blocks of time, but eight weeks has served us well. It is important to realize that the philosophical vision has to mesh well with the practical realities of running a school on a daily basis. Building administrators and classroom teachers appreciate this attentiveness, and it is important to take issues like this into consideration.

A final issue is one of intervention integrity. Throughout this book, we have emphasized that selecting one particular program or set of materials for a specific tier of RTI does not support the spirit of the philosophy. Teachers need to be given the freedom and flexibility to meet the needs of the students with whom they are working. Of course, as with any large institution, the freedom to self-select materials can lead to discrepancies in quality. To avoid this, the staff members who provide interventions to a student in any tier of the RTI model must complete an Intervention Fidelity form as shown in Chapter 9. This form asks the teacher to describe the intervention and indicate its frequency and duration. This information is collected and reviewed by the RTI team before making any decisions about movement between tiers. Completing this form reminds them that interventions must be provided with consistency and fidelity, even when the materials may differ between students.

Change is never easy, but it is often very advantageous for those brave enough to press forward. While implementing a Response to Intervention model in your district may seem overwhelming at times, it is well worth the investment of time and energy. It is not only a means to providing much needed assistance to struggling students, but also a mindset for looking at many of the issues plaguing public school systems across the country.

13

How Can I Apply RTI in Other Areas?

Throughout this entire book, the focus of the Response to Intervention model has been primarily on improving the literacy skills of elementary-age students. The Universal Screening and progress monitoring tools discussed have focused on the ability to develop fundamental reading skills, and most of the real-world vignettes have illustrated possible concerns related to the language arts curriculum. As an elementary school centered district, the emphasis on literacy makes a great deal of sense. Without the ability to read and communicate, subjects like mathematics, social studies, and science become immeasurably more difficult. That is why the Response to Intervention model was so attractive to the district in the first place. What we found however, was that we could easily apply the RTI model that we implemented to improve the pre-referral interventions available to our struggling readers to so many other areas of concern. It is important to look at the underlying philosophies of the model and apply them to the myriad of areas in which students need additional assistance.

When the Response to Intervention model is broken down into its simplest form, the components are applicable to almost any situation that requires outside assistance to solve. The heart of the model encourages early identification of the issue or problem, a research-based set of interventions or solution methods to utilize, a system to determine if the set of interventions or solutions has positive impacts on the issue or problem, and a set time limit to determine if you should make changes to unsuccessful interventions. When the model is explained in these terms, it is easy to apply to everyday tasks. Consider the analogy of a diet plan for unexpected weight gain. We all know it is best to identify the weight gain as quickly as possible and create a plan of attack. It is easier to correct the problem when it is at the ten-pound mark as opposed to when it reaches the 25-pound mark. We are also very aware that it is usually most effective to follow research-based diet plans as opposed to something more extreme and unproven. Following the simple outline above, weighing a person on a scale could help determine if the selected diet plan is having a positive impact, and a time-limit for a goal would be set. If the goal was not reached by the intended date, it would make sense to try something different for the next attempt. While this diet example may seem a bit humorous and out of place, it does illustrate the idea that we can apply the basics of RTI to any situation that needs intervention. The next step for educators is to think of ways they can apply it to other areas within their schools.

Behavior Modification and RTI

One of the easiest applications of the Response to Intervention philosophy is in behavior modification. Many students today have challenging behavior patterns that often lead them out of the regular education classroom and into the special education realm. While special education services are certainly necessary for some students, too often they are used as a crutch when successful behavior plans cannot be developed. In 1997, the IDEA legislation suggested that districts use Positive Behavior Support (PBS) to assist teachers with modifying the behaviors of challenging students. PBS is grounded in the idea that teachers use a Functional Behavioral Assessment (FBA) to accurately identify the issues about the behavior, and then they can develop an individual plan to change the behavior. Inherent in the plan are opportunities to monitor the progress of the arrangement, and reassess and change it as needed. The components of PBS mirror the basic philosophies of RTI and can be applied to behavior modification in any setting—special education or regular education, school-wide opportunities or a single classroom setting.

Think for a moment about a kindergarten or first grade classroom with a student who has difficulty raising his or her hand during classroom lessons. Obviously, this scenario plays out in thousands of classrooms every year. Many teachers have tried-and-true methods for combating this situation, and many are successful. The question becomes what to do in such situations when the teacher is not able to alter the student's behavior. Following the basic RTI principles, the teacher must first identify the problem. This is generally easy to do for most behavioral issues. The second step is to institute a set of research-based interventions. While this example of a student not raising his or her hand in class may not lead to extensive research opportunities, the interventions selected most certainly would be the result of personal experience. Monitoring the progress of the selected interventions is the next issue with which to contend. In this scenario, the teacher would need to consciously chart the number of times the student did and did not raise a hand. This data lets the teacher make an informed decision about whether the interventions selected were working adequately, or if there needed to be modifications made. Throughout this whole process, the teacher should establish definite timelines and communicate them to the child and the parents. This way, everyone is on the same page if additional measures must be introduced.

Of course this example is extremely simplistic, but it makes an extraordinarily valuable point. Any time an educator wants to address an issue in a classroom, he or she can apply RTI principles. Doing so takes the guess work out of the decision-making process and allows all the interested parties to have a clear picture of the identified problem, the interventions used, the ultimate goal being sought, and the timeline in which it is to be accomplished. In today's world of instant access to information and the perceived need for immediate results, this structure not only goes a long way in remediating the presenting issue, but it also strengthens the invaluable school-home communication link.

Other Academic Areas and RTI

Since we are an elementary school district, focusing on early literacy was most advantageous for us. Implementing systems and procedures that enabled students to secure the strongest literacy skills improved many areas in our schools because reading is such an essential component of all learning. As we saw before, you can apply the philosophies and principles that underscore the RTI model in many different areas, and this includes subject areas outside of elementary language arts literacy.

A story from our early experience with the Response to Intervention model makes this point very clear. It is important to remember that in the early stages of RTI, all staff members were asked to strictly adhere to the rules and procedures set forth by the committee; exceptions to these rules and procedures were unacceptable.

It is easy to understand how implementation of any new program can vary in a district with multiple schools and numerous building-level administrators. During the early days of the Response to Intervention movement, we were very specific about how students could progress to a Child Study Team referral. The rules were clear: If DIBELS (our Universal Screening tool of choice) did not pick up a primary-grade student who was not officially in a tier, there was no academic means of gaining access to a CST evaluation. The Intervention and

Referral Services (I&RS) Team would address behavioral concerns, but RTI was to address all academic issues.

A principal called the Assistant Superintendent of Curriculum and Instruction one day to discuss a primary grade student who was having difficulty in the area of mathematics. The Universal Screening had not identified the student in question as needing assistance, and the classroom teacher did not report significant reading problems. The child was not performing at grade-level in math, and the teacher believed that the root cause was a learning disability. The principal wanted to know how to proceed.

The two administrators started discussing ways to allow this child to have access to a CST evaluation. While this seems logical at first glance, the assistant superintendent finally stopped and asked the principal questions related to the core beliefs of RTI. What was the actual issue at hand? Did the problem stem from a lack of conceptual understanding, or was it that more rote mathematical issues could not be recalled? What types of interventions was the classroom teacher using? How was the classroom teacher assessing the effectiveness of these interventions? How would the teacher know when it was time to abandon these interventions and try something different in nature? While the answers to these questions were not as readily available in the area of mathematics as they were in language-arts literacy, they were still equally important. Until all research-based interventions had been tried and monitored for their success, there was no reason to go ahead with a Child Study Team evaluation that could lead to possible classification as a special education student.

The most difficult part of this scenario comes when it is time to talk to the classroom teacher about what needs to happen. The teacher often views a request to try more research-based interventions and monitor their progress as a means of avoiding the problem at hand. Many educators and parents can see the RTI process as an administrative design to delay CST testing and classification that, from their point of view, gets the students the assistance that they desperately need. In this case, as in many others in the district, the decision to follow an RTI-like protocol for a subject outside of language arts literacy benefitted the student because the child received the necessary extra help. It also benefitted the district, which avoided the need for a CST evaluation and possibly an unnecessary classification.

While these discussions with building-level administrators, teachers, and parents were not always easy, the RTI model does serve other academic areas well and should be followed whenever possible.

It is important to keep in mind the pitfalls that we face when trying to fully implement an RTI model in areas outside literacy. Finding an acceptable Universal Screening and progress monitoring tool leads the list of inhibiting factors. A Universal Screening tool needs to reliably predict future success in a given area, and it should be easy to administer and score. Without these two components, the benefits of an RTI model diminish very quickly. Our district has found it very challenging to find an adequate tool for use in the academic areas outside literacy, so at this point we just apply the philosophy without a strict flowchart of tiers.

Upper-Elementary Grades and Beyond

The same kinds of issues arise when applying the philosophies and beliefs of Response to Intervention to upper-elementary grades, as well as to middle and high school. The key to this transition is now easy to see: identify the problem as early as possible, use research-based interventions or solutions, monitor the progress of these interventions or solutions, and have a well-defined timeline for implementation and decision-making. Following these steps seems very logical at any grade level, but it is the logistics that become a little harder to manage.

The first pitfall is the same as the one mentioned for moving RTI into subject areas other than language-arts literacy. To follow the flowchart as we designed it, a quality Universal Screening and progress monitoring tool needs to be secured. Middle or high schools would need numerous tools because the subject areas become much more isolated and specific. A tool that would work well for a student struggling in Algebra 1 will not be useful for a student struggling in Biology. It is also more likely that a student is only struggling in one particular area as the grade level increases. In elementary school, the subject areas are so intertwined that, many times, a student's struggles in one area spill over to cause struggles in other areas as well. While this certainly can occur in the more departmentalized settings of middle and high school, it is not always the case. Regardless of the area of difficulty, it is critical to have a tool or procedure that identifies students who need additional assistance.

In the later grades, the acquisition of a specific tool for Universal Screening may not be possible or completely necessary. It is important to think about the benefits of screening all students three times a year as outlined in the RTI model presented. Instead, it might be most useful to use preexisting data about students suspected of needing extra help. Standardized state test scores, report card grades, common benchmark assessments, teacher observations, and the like can be gathered into a common reporting form that allows the RTI team to decide who receives the available additional assistance. By middle school, there is generally a wealth of data on each student.

Organizing this information and using it to make decisions seems much more economical in terms of time, cost, and effort than attempting to locate acceptable Universal Screening tools and administering them in all subject areas three times a year.

After students have been identified, the next obstacle to overcome is progress monitoring. Educators should use data to determine whether or not an intervention is working adequately. It is vital to the integrity of the RTI model to have this component in place. Benchmark assessments, common class-work assessments, or standardized testing options may serve this purpose well, but regardless of the tool selected, educators should identify appropriate target points. Progress monitoring is the essence of the Response to Intervention philosophy because it allows educators to make definitive, objective decisions about whether or not a practice works. Once the district decides what tool to use in this capacity, it can apply the RTI model in any grade and for any subject area.

Once you have satisfied the Universal Screening and progress monitoring components, the only remaining issue is determining which research-based interventions to use. Traditionally, the older grade levels have relied on intervention as a means to improve a student's classroom grades. In a true RTI setting, the goal of intervention is to remediate deficiencies with the understanding that classroom grades will improve as a result of this. Schools implementing an RTI model in middle and high school settings should investigate many intervention materials and make sure that the staff utilizing them has access to adequate, ongoing professional development.

Response to Intervention is a problem-solving model which districts can apply to a wide variety of settings. The key to its success is applying the basic principles in a way that works with the content area of focus. The issues you face will be different when you move from elementary school to middle school, or from language arts literacy to mathematics. As long as educators embrace the philosophy and adhere to the key components, student achievement will improve and the correct students will benefit the most from the intervention services available.

References

Allington, R. (2010, April 12). Responding to RTI. Interview by Anthony Rebora, *Education Week.*

Brown-Chidsey, R. & Steege, M. (2005). *Response to intervention: Principles and strategies for effective practice.* New York: The Guilford Press.

Buffam, A., Mattos, M., & Weber, C. (2009). *Pyramid response to intervention: RTI, professional learning communities, and how to respond when kids don't learn.* Bloomington, IN: Solution Tree Press.

Burns, M. & Gibbons, K. (2008). *Implementing response-to-intervention in elementary and secondary schools: Procedures to assure scientific-based practices.* New York: Routledge.

Fountas, G. & Pinnell, I. (1996). *Guided reading.* Porstmouth, NH: Heinemann.

Fuchs, L. S., Fuchs, D., Hosp, M. K., & Jenkins, J. R. (2001). Oral reading fluency as an indicator of reading competence: A theoretical, empirical, and historical analysis. *Scientific Studies of Reading, 5,* 239–256.

National Association of School Psychologists. (n.d.). *Research Summaries.* Retrieved December 2010 from http://www.nasponline.org/advocacy/researchsummaries.aspx

University of Oregon Center on Teaching and Learning. (n.d.). *DIBELS Data System.* Retrieved December 2010, from https://dibels.uoregon.edu/

U.S. Department of Education. (n.d.). *No Child Left Behind Act (NCLB).* Retrieved December 2010 from http://www2.ed.gov/nclb/landing.jhtml

U.S. Department of Education. (n.d.) *Building the Legacy: IDEA 2004.* Retrieved December 2010, from http://idea.ed.gov/

Wright, J. (2007). *Response to intervention toolkit: A practical guide for schools.* New York: National Professional Resources, Inc.; Dude Publishing.